THE ACTOR'S SURVIVAL KIT

THE ACTOR'S SURVIVAL KIT

by Miriam Newhouse
and Peter Messaline

Simon & Pierre
Toronto, Canada

We would like to express our gratitude to the **Canada Council,** the **Ontario Arts Council,** the **Book Publishing Industry Development Program** of the **Department of Communications,** and the **Ontario Publishing Centre** of the **Ministry of Culture, Tourism and Recreation** for their generous assistance and ongoing support.

Kirk Howard, President; Marian M. Wilson, Publisher

Simon & Pierre Publishing Co. Limited, a subsidiary of Dundurn Press

2 3 4 5 • 7 6 5 4
First edition 1990; second revised edition 1993

Canadian Cataloguing in Publication Data

Newhouse, Miriam, 1944–
   The actor's survival kit

ISBN 0-88924-216-X

1. Acting - Vocational guidance - Canada.
I. Messaline, Peter, 1944– . II. Title.

PN2055.N4 1990   792'.028'02371   C90-094062-X

General Editor: Marian M. Wilson
Editor: Peter Goodchild
Designer: Shawn Syms
Printed and bound in Canada by Metropole Litho Inc.

Order from Simon & Pierre Publishing Company Limited, care of

Dundurn Press Limited	**Dundurn Distribution**	**Dundurn Press Limited**
2181 Queen Street East	73 Lime Walk	1823 Maryland Avenue
Suite 301	Headington, Oxford	P.O. Box 1000
Toronto, Canada	England	Niagara Falls, N.Y.
M4E 1E5	OX3 7AD	U.S.A., 14302-1000

Contents

Introduction

"The last thing one knows when writing a book is what to put first."
– Pascal

This is a book about being an actor in Canada. It's not about how to act – there are plenty of ways to learn that – and it's not about working in the States – plenty of people have written about that. *The Actor's Survival Kit* is about the problems of being an actor, but it is mainly a celebration of the fact that so many people overcome those problems. If you are interested in being a professional actor in Canada, we are talking to you.

What makes us uniquely qualified to write this book? For one thing, we have made all the mistakes it is possible to make and we aren't afraid to pass them on to you as an Awful Warning. (As we continue to work and make new mistakes, we will probably bring out a sequel.) We have both worked in the United States, England and Canada and can talk about the business here from a broad perspective. Teaching acting as a business across the country, we have listened to the questions and concerns of hundreds of people in just your situation. More important, we have survived twenty-five years in the business (each) and are considered successful by our peers, if not by our families. ("When are you going to get a real job?")

When we moved to Canada, almost no one knew anything about us, good or bad. We had some good credits and more varied experience than most North American actors but we were starting with a clean slate. If we were going to eat, we had to attack the market place and become as well-known as our competition. We had to find out where we were and how to succeed. We made some strong choices and they paid off. Since 1977, we have worked in most of the major theatres – and many of the minor ones – across the country. We've lived on the Prairies and in Toronto; we've covered the styles of acting from the Stratford Festival (Peter) and the Shaw Festival (Miriam and Peter) through to dozens of radio, film and television gigs.

This book won't make you a success. What it will do is help you discover what success is. We have a friend who lives in a log cabin in northern B.C. and accepts a couple of theatre jobs a year. Another friend can't walk down the street without being recognized because of his television series. We know actors who work nine to five, doing commercial voice-overs and earning six figure incomes in complete obscurity. Which one is a success? All of them, of course. Deciding what you want is your first step to success.

We're not offering you a miracle method. If you are at the beginning of your career, we can save you some time. Instead of making your own mistakes, you can read about ours. If you are further along, you can bounce your ideas off ours and perhaps get ammunition for a specific problem.

There are no easy answers here. But there are some hard questions you should be asking yourself. We can't take legal or moral responsibility for your career – that's your job. We can show you some problems and offer some advice but the solutions are up to you.

We can only talk about what we know. Unfortunately, that has meant we have had to ignore the francophone side of the business. We hope that someone with knowledge and experience will fill the gap.

Writers have yet to solve the he/she/they hassle. We try to steer clear of the problem where possible but have decided to call directors "he" and stage managers "she" because that has been the usual pattern in our experience. "Actor" is generic.

We try to avoid jargon but the business is full of it – if the meaning of anything isn't clear, you should find it in the Glossary. Anything in *bold italic* type appears there, too.

INTRODUCTION TO THE SECOND EDITION

Although organizations have moved and changed their names, and major players have risen or fallen in the hierarchy, the larger picture hasn't changed. Women and visible minorities are still treated unfairly; actors as a group are still the biggest contributors to producers' funds, still one of the worst paid groups in the country – and still consider themselves blessed in their career choice.

We were blessed by the generosity of the hundreds of people we interviewed and by the support of Marian Wilson, Jean Paton and Peter Goodchild, of Simon & Pierre. The new edition relies on all those contributions and help from the staff and our fellow Councillors in Equity and ACTRA. We are happy to be working with Kirk Howard of Dundurn, whose enthusiasm got this new edition under way.

A rich man would never give anything to panhandlers. He would lend them a dollar and say, "Pass it on when you see someone who needs it." We had people who were our mentors in the early days whom we can never really thank. This is our way of passing on what we have been given.

Chapter One
Taking Charge

"You can't hope to be lucky – you have to prepare to be lucky."
– Timothy Dowd, NYPD

Raise your hand and repeat after us: "I hereby swear that whatever information or advice I receive from the authors, I remain in charge of my own career." In a profession where employment depends so much on other people's tastes and biases, it is easy to feel that we have no control over our own affairs. We do have control – not much, but some – and the sooner we start using it, the better.

Acting is not only an art, it is also a business. Too many actors disagree. They are artists and as such should not have to deal with everyday, mundane pursuits. "Rubbish!" we cry. There is no point in being an artist if you cannot practise your art. No matter how good you are, if you aren't working, who cares?

Certainly the actual execution of our craft demands an artistry and a sensitivity that is at odds with the grownup world of business. Eve Brandstein writes in *The Actor*: "Performing is childlike and joyous. Being an actor is a profession. You act from the Child. You do business from the Adult."

Being an adult means doing things you'd rather someone else did. It also means knowing what has to be done. The business side of acting involves three main responsibilities, and not one of them is any fun: decision-making, marketing, and self-discipline.

DECISION-MAKING

Throughout your career, you will have choices to make. Every time you make a choice, you open one door and leave another closed. You will never find out what was really behind that closed door. Whatever opportunities you might have had are lost to you. How do you choose? How will you know if your choice was right? Who do you blame if your choice was wrong? Let's take these questions one at a time.

How do you choose? Find out as much as you can about the problem. Talk to people with knowledge and experience. Don't assume their strong assertions are fact. Do your research. The more facts you have, the better your chances are of making an adult, informed decision. Don't deny your instincts. Don't let anyone else make the decision for you. However tempting it is to let your agent or your best friend or your mother (or even the authors) tell you what to do, do not yield. It is your career and your decision. You are the one who has to live with the results of the choice.

How will you know if your choice was right? You won't. It is impossible to predict what might have been. Why waste your time?

Who do you blame if your choice was wrong? You have already worked out the answer to that one, haven't you? That's right, you have no one to blame but yourself. That is why being an adult is such a drag. But why blame anyone? Once you have made your decision, regrets and recriminations simply get in the way of doing the job. Make the best of it, get on with it and learn from it.

MARKETING

Unlike people who sell products outside themselves – food, vinyl tiles, pets, packaged holidays – actors are their own products. You are selling the way you look, the way you sound, the way you move. You are, in a very real way, selling yourself. To do so effectively, you need a hide tough enough to bear constant rejection, and a sensitivity and vulnerability to do the job you have been trained to do. The reality is, if you don't have the first, you won't need the second.

You have to know your product as well as how to sell it to your market. Richard Nelson Bolles writes in *What Color Is Your Parachute?*: "The person who gets hired is not necessarily the one who can do the job best but the one who knows the most about getting hired."

Your market is any possible *engager*:

- Theatre – classical, *regional*, dinner, children's, summer, commercial, *alternative*, *fringe*, musical, lunchtime, *industrials*, specialist (audible/visible minorities, handicapped)
- Film – *feature*, documentary, *in-house* (training, industrials), student, independent
- Television – soap opera, sit-com, action, educational, made-for-TV movies
- Commercials – on-camera, voice overs
- Radio – drama, story-telling, docu-dramas

You can create your own market by seeing a gap (bored lunch-time crowds in the City Hall plaza) and filling it ("Brown Bag Theatre presents *Hamlet on Rye*"). You learn about your market by reading plays, watching movies and television, going to the theatre, talking to other actors, attending *workshops* and reading trade journals. Some of this is fun to do, some of it is a deadly bore, all of it is necessary.

What is your "product"? Your product is yourself, what you are and what you can do. It's easy enough to talk about what you can do but what are you? What is your image? Are you a personable young professional? Are you a troubled teen-ager? A street kid on drugs? A tough, aggressive entrepreneur? A sensitive waif? A wife and mother with a month-old baby? A young father on welfare? Please don't think we are talking about what you can act. We assume that any actor worthy of the name could play any of the above types, providing the sex and age were right. But what do you project? It is not easy to know how you come across to the rest of the world. Inside, you may feel like a delicate flower but if you weigh 350 pounds, have a five o'clock shadow by noon and turn the air blue with four letter words, you are unlikely to get cast as Ariel; go for Caliban.

Finding out what you project is never easy. When we look in the mirror, we exaggerate some things and minimize others, according to how we feel about ourselves. Talk to your friends and teachers; they can give you an idea. Ask what they see you cast as; that's sometimes easier for them to answer. Your agent, when you have one, has less reason to give you a polite lie and more knowledge on which to base professional advice.

You do not have to look or sound like the popular actors of the day. There are trends in actors as in everything else. Discover what makes you uniquely you. Bill Cosby, as quoted by Arsenio Hall: "I don't know the key to being successful. But the secret to failure is trying to be like everyone else."

Once you know the market and know your product, you have to be able to put the two together. Self-promotion is tedious and time-consuming. It is also essential. Ted Bairstow, Nova Scotia Department of Culture, in a personal letter to the authors: "[Young actors'] interest is in doing the thing and they have little advanced knowledge of what is required to, first, get the opportunity to do it and, second, support themselves by doing it." We are here to supply that knowledge. What you do with it is up to you.

Promotion means spending money. From a concert artist quoted in the Alberta Culture booklet, *Touring Attractions*: "I think one factor which slowed the beginning of my own career was my failure to recognize the legitimate need for an artist to invest a certain amount of money in promotional material ... I was under the mistaken impression that this was reprehensible, undignified, unfair to artists with even less financial resources. There are unavoidable costs involved in bringing one's name to the attention of prospective employers; there is no need to feel promotion means 'buying' a career."

Self-Discipline

Ted Bairstow: "[Graduates] ... lack the business and organizational skills to maintain the records and accounts necessary to function as self-employed individuals." The authors feel that actors don't so much lack the skills as think them unimportant.

You have to spend time and energy working to find work. There is not much excitement in keeping files up to date, even less joy in writing engagers, casting directors and agents, and few laughs in being put on hold by endless receptionists. Trudging off to an aerobics class in a blizzard can rate somewhere just short of root canal treatment. Logging phone conversations and jotting down theatre *seasons* are not right up there with curtain calls and great *reviews* but they are far more frequent. Thriller writer Dick Francis had this to say about jockeys, which we could have said about actors: "The grind, the frustration, the constant failures, the long hours and the poor pay aren't obstacles in the way of the job. They *are* the job. The applause, the big fee, the award, the triumph – all these are simply occasional bonuses to be enjoyed when they happen."

"There's No Business Like Show Business"

Very true. In other businesses you start at or near the bottom and work your way up. You probably won't reach the top but you move steadily towards it. In the business of acting you can start at any point on the ladder and spend your whole career climbing up and down. That is a puzzling, not to say foreign, concept for most people. You may be lucky enough to leave drama school and go straight into a leading role in a feature film or at a prestigious theatre (don't hold your breath) and after that ten-week contract not work again for the next eighteen months. More likely, your first job will come after several months, you will earn $165 in a morning on a radio drama followed by another six-month bout of unemployment. It has nothing to do with talent. It can't be foreseen. Success does not breed success.

Success does, however, breed self-confidence. So does knowledge. Having a clear understanding of what you have to do in the job market, and the tools you need to do it with, will give you that confidence.

The courage you will need to get through the next chapter you'll have to find for yourself. Read on.

Chapter Two
Gloomy Reality

"Fie upon this quiet life! I want work."
– Shakespeare

C aution: The career of acting contains insecurity, unemployment and rejection and is hazardous to your health." Unfortunately, acting addicts, like cigarette addicts, ignore the warnings and insist on continuing the habit. So we will not try to put you off with gloomy admonitions; we will simply present the facts. Here are the professional realities that you will encounter. At the end of the chapter, if you haven't given up in despair, you will have a better idea of the hurdles you face. The rest of the book shows you how to clear them.

You did not decide to become an actor worrying that statistically you are likely to fail. We don't say to ourselves, "I'm going to work and strive, sacrifice and persevere, so that one day I can look at myself in the mirror and say, 'I didn't make it.'" We all believe that we are going to be the successful ones, the ones who will beat the odds. Here's what those odds are.

MONEY

Here are the latest available facts and figures.
From Revenue Canada, 1991:

- The average Canadian earned income $32,850

We can assume that union actors make more than non-union actors:

- In 1992, the average acting income of an actor
  belonging to both unions $13,300
- Taking out those who made no money at all in 1992 $16,255

To give an idea of where we stand in the world at large:

- In 1991, crop farm workers average income $16,191
- In 1991, sewing machine operators average income $16,540

There are performers, even in Canada, who earn over $150,000 a year, but they are a minute proportion of the acting population. If you are planning to go into the acting business for the big bucks, think again. You will be doing unusually well if you support yourself by your acting alone.

UNEMPLOYMENT

All actors experience the seesaw of long, intense periods of work followed by great gaps of unemployment. From having had a structure and a meaning to your day imposed upon you, you are now faced with long hours of nothing. It is difficult to structure your unemployed time. You will have a flurry of activity where you are going to auditions every day, followed by long silences where you keep checking your phone for the dial tone.

Not only were those periods of work gratifying to your artistic ego, they also paid your rent. It is easy to fool yourself into thinking that the $200 or $450 or $1,500 you get per week or day is going to continue forever. It never does. It lasts as long as the job.

Here are some figures from performers' unions for work in union jurisdiction:

- Out of 4,700 paid-up members of Equity, around 1,000 are employed in any week.
- In 1992, 38% of Equity members did no work in theatre.
- Out of 10,000 ACTRA members, 1,500 to 2,000 work regularly.
- In 1992, 27% of ACTRA Toronto Performer members did no work on ACTRA contracts.
- In 1992, 20% of joint ACTRA/Equity members didn't act at all.

Acting work doesn't qualify for unemployment benefits in Canada. You can of course work (as a waiter, say), pay UIC premiums and claim UIC benefits when out of work. We used to have the same benefit but lost it in 1972 and have been trying to get it back ever since. Don't hold your breath.

Comparisons

If you think you have a better chance in the United States, think again. Lehman Engel, in *Getting Started in Theatre*, advises that a person of normal weight and height, with good vocal or dance technique, and some ability in the other skills, with something special to offer that few others have, will find it normal to attend classes regularly; go to sixteen Broadway and thirty off-Broadway auditions in one season, plus all the summer theatre auditions; send pictures and *résumés* to stage managers of all the shows (for replacement casting) – and get no work. Certainly, there are more jobs with very high fees in the States, but the competition for any work at all is intense.

From 1990–91 U.S. Equity official figures:

- In any week, 87% of U.S. Equity membership don't work in theatre.
- In any year, 59% of the membership don't work in theatre.
- The average member worked 16.9 weeks in the year.
- Median earnings of U.S. Equity membership was $4,934.

From Equity/Screen Actors' Guild surveys:

- 75 percent of members earn less than $2,500/year in union jurisdiction.
- 3 percent of members earn more than $25,000/year in union jurisdiction.

SEX

No, we haven't finally got to the good stuff. Women get a bad deal in most careers – underpaid for the same work, less access to senior jobs – and things aren't changing quickly, regardless of the lip service being given to equality. There is every reason why our profession should be free of this unfairness, but read on and weep. From the *Applebaum-Hébert Report* (1982): "We should like to draw special attention to the fact that the present inequitable access of women to all positions of responsibility and activity in the cultural sector deprives Canadian society as a whole of a vital dimension of human and artistic experiences."

- Women are 52 percent of the Canadian adult population.
- They form 40 percent of ACTRA membership overall.
- They form 35 percent of ACTRA membership earning over $12,000 a year.
- They form 30 percent of ACTRA membership earning over $30,000 a year.

The 1980 StatsCan *Survey of Performing Artists* showed that fewer women work all the time than men, that women are half again as likely to give up their career for a year or more at a time, and make on average about three quarters as much as men. This is actually better than Canadian women in general, who make two-thirds as much as men from full-time jobs (from a 1993 StatsCan report on 1990 incomes).

Rina Fraticelli surveyed the Playwrights Canada catalogue in 1981 and found only 36% of the plays had casts where the women outnumbered or were equal to the men. Our latest catalogue, which is three times larger, has exactly the same figures and shows twice as many male roles as female. A 1992 survey shows Equity women make significantly less than men throughout their careers, except in the 20–25 age range.

The situation is the same in ACTRA. Twice as many men as women earn over $30,000 from ACTRA contracts and 80% of voice overs are done by men. In 1983, a CRTC survey of Canadian advertising showed women characters were helpful and secondary rather than expert and decisive. Ten years later, Diana Platts, chair of the National ACTRA Women's Committee, is still fighting the same bias.

Mary Beth Hurt said in 1992, "You're an adolescent until you're 25, you're 25 until you're 40, and at 40 you slowly begin to disappear."

VISIBLE MINORITIES

Men have a professional advantage over women. Similarly, there is still an assumption that a character is white, central Canadian and "able" unless there is a note specifying otherwise. We are seeing this note more often on casting breakdowns but actual casting decisions haven't changed much in five years. There is a far smaller proportion of visible minorities on stage and screen than in society.

As a profession, we are beginning to fight back. ACTRA and Equity both have Equal Opportunities committees. Equity held the first national symposium on non-traditional casting and published the transcript, *Talent Over Tradition*. ACTRA publishes *Into the Mainstream*, a directory of performers in visible and audible minorities, or with handicaps. Sandi Ross, Chair of ACTRA's National and Toronto Equal Opportunities Committees, and driving force behind the initiative: "Visible minorities will be 17.7% of Canada's population in 2001 (45% in Toronto) and yet make up only three to six percent of on-screen casting."

There is a continuous spectrum of physical ability in the real world, from Olympic athletes to quadriplegics. Six percent of

Canada's working population is registered handicapped. How many characters have you seen who aren't able-bodied? In our business, as elsewhere, the wheelchair-bound are thought incapable of expressing themselves physically. However, the physically handicapped are beginning to fight the same battles being fought by ethnic groups.

It is difficult for women to be cast in parts where gender is irrelevant, or for a visible minority actor to be cast in a part where it is possible, but not necessary, to be Hispanic or Japanese or very short or unable to walk. Meg Hogarth, executive director of Media Watch, says that their new survey of Canadian series television indicates that women of colour are still underrepresented and stereotypically portrayed.

It is simply illegal to specify any gender, physical or racial type unless the part demands it and the new ACTRA Commercials Agreement sets up a bipartisan Equal Opportunities Committee to monitor this. So far so good, but in a recent survey, advertising producers thought that 21% of the public would object to visible minorities in commercials whereas only 4% actually did.

Pressure is being brought on engagers to spread out into non-traditional casting. Jini Stolk, Executive Director, Toronto Theatre Alliance, in *Canadian Theatre Review* lists four generally recognized types of non-traditional casting:

- Societal Casting: Using ethnic and female actors in roles they commonly play in society – doctors, lawyers, business people – rather than traditional roles of servant, etc.
- Cross-cultural Casting: Transferring the entire world of the play to another society ("The Black Mikado").
- Conceptual Casting: Casting an ethnic actor in order to bring a new resonance and nuance to a play.
- Colour-blind Casting: Casting totally without regard to race or ethnicity.

An actor from a minority has to ask: Do I want to be thought of simply as an actor? Do I want to be specifically black (or deaf or Hawaiian)? Do I want to be involved with companies made up of my type (Native Earth, Rolling Thunder)? There is no single right answer.

LOCATION

Actors tend to think that it is necessary to live in a large city in order to "make it" in the *business*. Up to a point, this is true. You are not going to have a particularly busy career if you base yourself in Moose Jaw or Moncton. On the other hand, you don't have to live in Toronto, Vancouver or Montreal in order to have a "successful" career.

Halifax, Saskatoon, Edmonton and Winnipeg have a range of theatres and fringe festivals, far more than one would imagine, given their size. Regina and Fredericton have the only two truly regional theatres in the country. The Maritimes have some of the most exciting indigenous theatre in North America. Calgary and Edmonton also have a media industry – not nearly as large as that in the three main cities, but then the pool of actors is much smaller.

The choice of where you want to make your base is up to you and depends on what is most important to you. With stage work, your choices are wide open. If you are born, raised and educated on the Prairies, you might want to stay there. You have your personal ties there and any professional contacts you have are likely to be in the area. However, if you want specifically to work in film and television, you will have to choose Vancouver or Toronto (or possibly Calgary). Although Montreal has a healthy film and television industry, you have to be a francophone to survive.

Some people, once they have decided on a base, are loath to leave it. A few, a very few, are able to survive in one place without working out of town. In any city apart from Toronto, this has the major danger that only a handful of engagers know your work first-hand and when two or three move out, as will happen eventually, you will be an unknown has-been. Most actors understand that although they may no longer be rogues, they are still vagabonds, and resign themselves to a travelling life.

LUCK

From Statistics Canada's *Survey of Performing Artists*: "Full-time involvement in the acting profession ... can be the product of many factors besides the individual's skill. Not the least of these is luck. Where one actor may find his working schedule filling with *engagements* which neatly and rapidly succeed each other, another actor, equally regarded, will spend substantial periods out of work because he has to decline offers which conflict with engagements for which he has already been contracted. The latter case is probably typical of the experience of most of those trying to make acting a full time profession." We see actors who float from job to job, easily dovetailing the end of one into the beginning of the next without lifting a finger. We work diligently at the business side of our careers and lose out on jobs because the director decided to cast a redhead or the writer changed the sex of the role. Knowing that luck has so much to do with employment is not a comfort. It is a danger. It tempts us to give up actively working for our careers.

REJECTION

In the course of a year, you may be turned down for literally scores of jobs. You will get work from about one audition in ten. Actors are not usually turned down because they aren't good enough. They are turned down because they aren't tall enough or young enough or fat enough. They are turned down because they remind the director of his ex-wife. They are rarely told why they have been rejected. And after each rejection, they have to go through the process all over again. It is easy to take that kind of rejection personally. After all, what is being rejected? Not your work record, not a product, but you. Your body, your voice, your face. At least that is how it feels (see page 68).

All these pressures take their toll on the human psyche. Actors fall into the all-too-easy trap of negativity and anger. They don't use the empty hours to go to workshops and classes, work out, read plays, go to the theatre, get involved in union activities, create new projects for themselves. They find it easier to sleep late, watch television, drink, and complain to anyone who will listen that if there were any justice, they would be down in L.A. working – nay, starring – in films.

Sorry, we seem to have started preaching. No warnings, just facts. Okay ... Dr. M. Plant, in the *British Journal on Alcohol and Alcoholism*: "People in artistic and literary occupations are peculiarly susceptible to alcoholism and by extension to other forms of over-indulgence in mood-changing drugs. Five major studies or surveys from England, Scandinavia and America show entertainers are at high risk." Out of nine high-risk factors in one of the studies, six are applicable to actors.

Occupations with maximum risk of heart disease are those with low power to control the job and high psychological strain. Sound familiar?

We could go on, but you've probably got the message by now. All right, you know what the odds are. Let's get to work on shortening them.

Chapter Three
Working to Get Work

"Nothing is more common than unsuccessful men of talent."
– Calvin Coolidge

Actors spend more time looking for work than they do working. They spend about 45 percent of their expenses after food and rental on self-promotion. It is boring, depressing and difficult, but it has to be done. *People* magazine: "As an actor, your real job is job hunting." However good you are, however well-toned your body and well-honed your craft, if nobody knows who you are or what you do, you won't get hired. Actors who don't believe in the necessity of promotion may find themselves overtaken by less talented actors who do.

Be practical, business-like and efficient in your search for work. Keep files with names, addresses and phone numbers of anybody and everybody who is a possible link to a job. You don't need a computer programme to do this. A three-ring binder is quite sophisticated enough, provided you keep it up to date. Put in details of interviews, information you get from radio, television or newspaper items. Make a note of phone conversations. Write down when you wrote, what you said. Write it down straight away. Keep in mind an old Persian proverb: "Fortune is infatuated with the efficient."

Don't decide too soon to concentrate on one area. Actors need every source of work they can get. Scott Hylands (of *Night Heat* and twenty-five years of theatre): "The boldness and breadth of a stage performance enlivens the work you do on film and television. The subtleties of film and television acting give detail and texture to your work on stage. One format informs the other." By focusing on only one area of the business, you are cutting off opportunities to expand both your career and your bank balance.

Spread your net wide. Keep in touch with people across the country. You may not change your home base, but other people do. Artistic directors constantly move from one city to another. You never know who is going to pop up where and in what hat. Ron Ulrich became the artistic director of Muskoka Summer Theatre, after six years of running the Stage West dinner theatre chain. Jackie Maxwell started the Atelier Theatre at the NAC, Ottawa, and is now artistic director of Toronto's Factory Theatre. James Roy was an artistic director in Victoria and Winnipeg before becoming executive producer of Stereo Drama in Toronto. Naturally, you will concentrate on the likeliest and the closest engagers but try not to cut anyone off completely. You never know when a contact is going to pay off.

The best time to look for work is when you don't have to – when you are still working. That is the time to pick up the bits of information that float around backstage or on a set. Chatting to make-up and wardrobe people can generate all sorts of useful news. You will be able to invite people to attend your show or watch your film. Going to an audition when you have work, you give off a confidence and ease that is hard to fake and attractive to see.

INITIAL INVESTMENT

You've got to spend money to make money. When it comes to large capital purchases, there is never any need to buy a new, full-price anything. Look through bargain hunter newspapers, scan notice boards in laundromats, seek out garage sales, or be truly courageous and brave Boxing Day sales.

The most important piece of equipment for an actor is a telephone. Without a phone, you are unreachable. And if they can't reach you, they can't hire you. The phone must be manned every minute of the day, which means you need an answering service, answering machine or Call Answer, the phone service voice mail utility.

Answering services run around $85 a month for answering on their number in regular business hours, more if they will intercept calls to your number. In any large city, there is often one company giving an amazing deal. Ask other actors which they use.

Answering machines are the cheapest option. Shop around and for less than $50 you'll find a basic two-cassette machine, with remote control so that you can call in for messages. Remember to call in if you're out for more than a few hours.

The Call Answer service from your phone company offers callers voice mail when you don't answer the phone – and also when you are busy with another caller. It costs around $5 a month, plus a one-time installation charge, and is available in larger centres.

A typewriter is a must. You will need to type your résumé (see Chapter Four, "Show and Tell") and all your letters to engagers and casting directors. You don't necessarily have to own one, but you must have access to one. It can't be any old clunker of a machine. It has to do a neat, professional job. Now that electronic typewriters and word processors are so popular, you can buy an ordinary electric typewriter for very little money. Second-hand ones are even cheaper.

If you cannot or will not type and can't get anyone else to do it for you, there are typing services available. For only slightly less than a king's ransom (minimum $30 an hour), you can pay someone else to do your clerical work.

Invest in a portable cassette recorder. Although a portable recorder will not give you as good a tone as a larger, more elaborate machine, it is more convenient for travelling. Recording your lines, listening to accent tapes and taping your own, learning lines and rehearsing audition speeches are activities which are best done in private. A small machine of your own with an earphone can avoid household rows and allow you to be independent of flatmates or parents.

It may sound strange but a television set and, to a lesser extent, a VCR are two more pieces of essential equipment for an actor. If you are going to be doing any television work, you have to learn about the market. You have to keep abreast of the new programmes, directors and other actors. Find out what is popular, what sells. Keep in touch with trends. If the casting director describes the programme as a "Street-Legal-type show," you should know what that means. If you are told that it's a regular beer commercial, that should mean something to you. A VCR is useful for taping important programmes that you are unable to watch.

If you are a member of a performers' union, buy space in *Face to Face with Talent*. This is a national directory of union actors, with their names, photographs, agents and recent work credits. Your local ACTRA office (see Addresses, pages 194 to 202) probably puts out a similar smaller-scale directory. Being listed with these is worth the cost. They are well-respected and distributed free to engagers in film, television, radio, commercials and theatre. Engagers have been using *Face to Face* for years and you can be pretty sure that in the long run it will pay back your listing cost in the work you gain.

If you qualify for inclusion, *Into the Mainstream* is the directory of ACTRA and Equity performer members in audible or visible minorities, or with handicaps. Engagers do look here for specific types. As far as we have seen, other print directories have not been worthwhile, except for the booklets some talent agencies put out to publicise their clients.

Computer casting directories should work but have not so far. Theoretically, being able to list actors with specific abilities for would-be engagers should be a service worth money to both actors and engagers. Unfortunately, no one has yet been able to get together enough actors and enough engagers at the same time.

All right, you have all your equipment, now what do you do with it? How do you actually go about looking for work? How do you get to meet engagers and casting directors? How do you find out about auditions? What do you do after you have found out?

RESEARCH

Before you start writing letters, phoning or pounding the pavement, find out as much as you can about the people you want to meet and the places where you want to work. Engagers are looking for solutions to their problems. You have to find out what their current problems are. What's the show? What's uncast? You cannot write an effective letter or show yourself off well at an interview if you are whistling in the dark. Brian Levy, casting director: "Know what's going on – read the *trades*, know who's who. Have up-to-date lists of directors and theatres with their seasons. Make notes on people you've seen and written to."

You have dozens of sources of information. All addresses of organizations mentioned below are listed in the Addresses section, page 194. The Professional Association of Canadian Theatres (PACT) publishes a directory of Canadian professional theatres, with addresses and other information. Go to the theatre itself. Phone the box office for the new season's plans. Pick up a brochure. Attend some plays. Read the artistic director's notes in the programme. If the theatre is out-of-town, write for a brochure. Do they perform middle-of-the-road material or is it all experimental? Is their season essentially Canadian or is it a mix of Canadian, American and European? Do they produce all, some or any new plays? Musicals? Classical? Does their *studio* space have a separate director you should write to?

There are information notice boards at the Equity offices in Vancouver and Toronto. Equity newsletters are sent to members, some libraries and drama schools. They contain audition dates and times, and new appointments.

Equity also has an up-to-date theatre *management* list free for its members. Read *Theatrum, Canadian Theatre Review*, and other theatre magazines, available on newstands or by subscription.

There are PUC (Playwrights' Union of Canada) reading rooms across the country, where you can read a copy of the PUC newsletter. This publication, which comes out six times a year, lists theatre seasons across the country and has information on Canadian playwrights. Get it at a major public library or write for a subscription. Learning about film and television is easy. Watch them. Find out what the market is. Buy the trade magazines. *Playback*, out of Toronto and published every two weeks, is a national magazine with reviews and information about upcoming productions, including their casting directors. Most major centres have their own media periodicals and directories, which you can find in local libraries and in your local ACTRA office. The ACTRA offices have lists of local media engagers and casting people.

Newspapers, both local and national, are good sources of information. For Toronto-based actors, Gaylyn Britton's *Getting Organized* is a handy-dandy directory.

Agents, engagers and casting directors like to know that you care enough about them to do some research. You are paying them a compliment. Don't try to use all you know at the interview but let it give you an air of competence. It will help you keep control, you won't waste time and the interviewer will know you are serious and professional.

NETWORKING

Networking goes on in every business and in every part of life. It involves casual and not-so-casual personal contacts. It is meeting people, talking, trading information. Nicholas Rice, actor, in the *Globe and Mail*: "When I saw unemployment looming, I sent chatty cards to everyone – to agents, directors, producers – telling them I would soon be free ... I would sit in this lobby, that green room, this office, until someone would come over to chat. I learned a lot this way: it's called networking. But it all takes time ... I had not always been able to network [in Vancouver] ... So, persevere. Pound the pavement. Continue to make at least one call and one personal visit a day. Send out at least one letter. Keep your ear to the ground, and ask as many people as you can, 'What's happening?'"

Some actors frequent actors' pubs. Some acting communities have local newsletters and regular get-togethers. Fitness clubs, workshops, seminars and classes are used, not just for the professional skills that you gain, but for the conversations that can lead to information about auditions, new productions, who is leaving what management and going where. Don't forget about directors and stage managers. They like to talk, too, and often hear things before actors do.

Networking is a two-way street. There is no advantage to be gained by hoarding news about a change of artistic directors at a theatre or an audition for a new film. Giving that information out to someone else won't hinder your chances of getting a job. Be as generous with your information as you would like others to be with theirs. It will come back to you a thousand-fold.

Be sensitive in your networking. No director wants to be hounded about work at a party. Make sure that you are behaving in an appropriate manner for the situation. (We don't expect you to turn to a fellow pallbearer and whisper, "So, doing any casting?" but we have heard stories nearly that bad.)

Some people find this kind of promotion the easiest and most natural. Others find it a strain and a bore. Go with your strengths. If kibbitzing in a bar with other theatricals is a piece of cake, go for it. If not, try to do *some* but concentrate on writing letters and phoning friends.

LETTERS

Canada Post can get in where the actor can't. Letters are the most practical way of introducing yourself.

There are a few general rules:

- The letter should look professional. Plain white bond paper, typed clearly in black, with adequate margins, centred on the page.
- The letter should be short. The fewer words you send, the more chance you have that every word will be read. Besides, if you say it all in the letter, what are you going to talk about in the interview?
- Make sure the letter has your full name, return address and phone number on it.
- Be direct and natural. Your letter should be business-like without being stiff and formal. Write the way you would talk at an interview – use contractions, avoid business clichés.
- Stress the positive; omit the negative.
- "Dear Sir or Madam" is death. We know people who see that and chuck the letter unread. Use the person's name. And *spell it right*.
- Avoid being aggressive, familiar or "cutesy." You are writing to a stranger about something that is important to

you both. Even if you are writing to someone you know very well, keep the tone professional. There are some engagers and casting directors who don't mind slightly off-the-wall correspondence, but unless you know who they are, it isn't worth taking the risk.

• Don't concentrate on how wonderful an opportunity this would be for *you*. Engagers are more interested in how hiring you will help *them*.

Margaret Mooney, artistic co-ordinator, Citadel Theatre, Edmonton: "Tell me the specific role you're interested in. Be sure you're right. Read the play! Drop me a postcard. Tell me your availability. Don't ask me for advice about your career; I'm not your agent. Don't badger me; if you ask and I put your name forward and the director won't see you – tough."

Stuart Aikins, casting director: "I like getting pertinent information in letters from actors; career developments, performances in town, media work. I won't go to see you in a show but the topic may come up in a conversation with someone. Actors do disappear if they don't keep in touch. They slip through the cracks. Don't give your own opinion of your work. What actor is going to say he's bad? But including other people's opinions in reviews is a good way to let me know."

Peter Mandia, artistic director, Theatre Aquarius, Hamilton: "I like to be kept in touch; it's nice to be thought of. Don't send a résumé and photograph with nothing else. You should have an accompanying letter. At least self-publicity shows an active interest. Commitment can outweigh talent."

A Toronto casting director: "By all means send notes. They are no intrusion. But be specific! There's no point in saying, 'I have just been working in Halifax and have done some commercials and would like to do more.' What were you doing in Halifax? What commercials have you done? What sort of commercials are you best suited for? Give me something to go on."

The Letter of Introduction

This letter accompanies your résumé and photograph. Like all the letters you write, it should be short and direct. The letter should give a feeling of enthusiasm without hysteria, confidence without arrogance and modesty without diffidence. Easy, eh?

Find a selling point. Why should this busy casting director see you? What do you have that makes you especially useful? That is what promotion is all about. How can you solve the engager's problems?

Find a hook to hang the letter on. If you are in a show, extend an invitation. Most casting directors keep abreast of films and plays. One casting director told us that the only films he misses are sci-fi and teenage romps. "I go to the theatre a minimum of two nights a week. First because I enjoy it, second to see the *talent*. I want to stay current." Brian Levy: "During the season, I probably see three plays a week. I watch as much TV and go to as many films as possible." If you know that the engager was recently at one of your school productions, mention that and the role you played. If you have a mutual acquaintance with some clout, ask if you can say, "So-and-so suggested that I write to you." If nothing else, suggest that a meeting will be useful to transform you from a picture and résumé into a flesh and blood human being.

Always end with a specific next step. "I look forward to hearing from you" is vague and useless. "I'll call your office next Monday to set up a time to meet" is positive and gives you a second chance of being in touch. (Many directors will not see actors if there is no specific reason, such as casting a show or general auditions. The only way to find out is to try.)

The Letter for Specific Casting
In a way, this letter is easier to write. You want something particular, to be considered for a definite role, and the letter is to say why you should be considered. Do not concentrate on what you will gain from the experience but on what you have that makes you hireable. To be hired, even to be considered seriously, you have to use what makes you different from other actors.

Keeping in Touch
This is the only letter that doesn't start "Dear So-and-so." The envelope is still addressed to a specific person but the letter inside is mainly a general newsletter. You should be sending this sort of letter every few months, just to let people know what you have been doing, what you are doing now or what you are going to be doing. Its basic purpose is to get your name on the desk and into active consideration. (In February, just before they hold auditions, you might send one to all the summer theatres with news of your winter.) Try to add a specific comment for each recipient, as a sort of personal postscript. ("Dear Fred Belville, congratulations on your forty-fifth season at Malmaison.") Tina Gerussi, Toronto

casting director: "It's always a good thing to drop off a note to casting directors to let them know what you've been doing and if you're going to be in a show. Your agent won't necessarily do it."

Some theatre directors will tell you they do not want this type of letter. If so, don't send it. The authors feel that a "keeping in touch" note three times a year is not excessive. There are those who would disagree.

PHONE CALLS

Before you know someone well, a cold phone call is a dangerous thing. You can't know how busy the office is when you call and you are likely to get the polite runaround from a secretary. From one casting director: "I dislike direct phone contact. If I have three lines busy, a *client*, an agent and an actor, guess which one I'm not going to get to?" Write first, saying you will call.

Before you lift the receiver, write down as much as you need to be sure you will cover all the necessary points. Not a script but every single important fact and name. Treat the call as an audition – the Confident Professional – rehearse it out loud, with a friend if you like.

Once on the phone, introduce yourself and ask to speak to the engager or casting director. If the receptionist or secretary asks you why, don't stumble, mumble or ramble. Have a capsule reason why the engager should take your call: "It concerns the upcoming *Hamlet* casting," or "It's to arrange an interview. I wrote to Ms. Blank saying that I would phone today." If the person is busy, ask when would be a good time to call back. If the secretary says that the engager will return your call, simply leave your name and number – no long message. If you are not successful first time, get the secretary's name so that next time your call can be more personal. Getting the secretary on your side can make all the difference.

Once you have got through to the correct person, make sure you introduce yourself, even if you have already done so to the secretary. Do not assume your name will ring any bells; refer to your letter. State clearly and confidently what you want. It shouldn't be difficult. You've got your notes right in front of you. Do not prolong the call. Once the business is over – you've got an appointment, you're to call back next week – reconfirm the information and finish.

If the engager or casting director does not return your call, call back. You will have to use your own judgement about how soon to do this. And how often.

Never phone a casting director or an agent at home. Ever. Unless asked.

PERSONAL VISITS

There is no question that a ten-minute visit is worth ten thousand written words. Make the most of it; you are not likely to get any longer. There is at least one casting director who says that if he does have the time to see actors, he sees them for five (count 'em, five) minutes. He will give them 100 percent of his complete and undivided attention but five minutes is all they get.

Knowing that you have only a limited time, how do you use it most effectively? Why are you there? What do you want to say about yourself? What do you want to gain? If this is just an introductory interview, be prepared to talk about anything. Make life easy for the interviewer. Reply fully and show your interest.

Don't be afraid to disagree; there is nothing wrong with having an opposing opinion. A director is more likely to remember a lively dispute than a bland acceptance. But be careful how you express yourself; angry confrontation is not attractive.

Don't be afraid to admit ignorance. No one is going to expect you to know everything. Besides, people enjoy explaining things to others.

Don't monopolize the conversation. It's far more interesting for both parties to take an active role in the interview. On the other hand, avoid "yes" and "no" answers. This is your time to show what sort of person you are. You've only got ten minutes; use them.

When it's time to leave, leave. Learn to read body language. Keep your antennae working. You won't gain anything by trying to prolong an interview that has come to a natural end.

After the interview, which should end with a smile and a thank you, drop the interviewer a quick note of thanks. It is polite and it puts your name on the desk once more in a legitimate fashion.

Make a note in your files of what you discussed, so that the next time you meet you will be able to pick up the conversation and build on it.

PERSISTENCE

Promoting yourself through letters, visits, phone calls and social contacts is not a one-shot deal. Self-publicity is an on-going activity. Engagers and casting directors hear from actors and their agents daily. Ensure that you don't get lost in the shuffle – not through constant badgering but through a relaxed, professional, individual approach.

TALENT BANKS

The largest Talent Bank in the country, the CBC's Talent Resource Centre (see Addresses, page 199), has over ten thousand union and non-union actors on file. It is used by the CBC and freelance media directors, and by theatres who are looking for performers with specific skills. The file includes the performer's address, phone number, agent, a physical description and special skills (sports, musical instruments, singing, dancing, foreign languages, accents). As well as the computer database, the Resource Centre holds artists' *demo* tapes (see Chapter Four, "Show and Tell"), TV drama tapes and scripts, and a clipping file. Actors are encouraged to call in, add reviews to their files, replace their old photographs and résumés, and make sure their contact number and availability are up to date. Across the country, there are other Talent Banks. CBC in Vancouver has one, as does ACCESS-TV (the educational channel) in Edmonton. Keeping your name and information on file gives you one more chance of being cast.

Talent Banks have one thing in common that makes them one of the most popular forms of promotion: *they're free!*

SHOWCASES

Let people know when you are working. It is the best way of introducing yourself to an engager or casting director. Casting directors agree: "Actors should be involved in *showcase* productions. It's a great way to remind us that you're around. No matter where you are in the hierarchy, do something constructive and visible. Recognize the power and importance of visibility and take advantage of it." Many directors will attend community theatre productions if the quality of the work is known to be good. In Toronto, Equity Showcase productions are at least as popular as "real" shows and use both union and non-union actors. If you have some time, money and friends in a like situation, mount your own production. It may be expensive, but you are making an investment in your professional future. Fringe festivals now flourish across the country from Victoria to Halifax, making it easier to mount your own showcase.

Directors and casting people are intensely interested in new talent, but however good you are, if no one knows about your talent, you won't work. They won't beat a path to your door if they don't know where you live.

Chapter Four
Show and Tell

"God has given you one face and you make yourself another."
– Shakespeare

Your promotion is only as effective as the materials you use. The two most important weapons in your publicity armoury are your résumé and your photograph. They encapsulate in a nine-by-twelve envelope just what it is you are selling. The résumé shows at a glance where you trained, who trained you, your height, weight and colouring, your union status, your stage and media experience and your special skills. Your photograph gives an idea of your age range, your image and your personality. Not bad for nine inches by twelve inches.

Directors, producers, casting people and agents are bombarded with photographs and résumés from hopeful actors. These packages arrive in the mail, they are shoved under doors, they accompany actors to auditions. How can you ensure that your little publicity package will be remembered? You can't. What you can do is ensure that it won't be tossed out without a glance. However exciting and frequent your work has been, it will not even be looked at if it is presented on a wrinkled piece of paper, badly typed and poorly photocopied. In this business, the form is as important as the content.

RÉSUMÉS

Your résumé is a summary of your training and experience to date. Everything in your résumé should earn its space. There are several books on the market that discuss what makes an effective résumé and there are résumé services that will create a résumé for you. Although the books have some interesting and useful ideas and most of the résumé services are reliable, they use a standard format which fits most clients' needs. They rarely understand the actor's specific requirements. A standard résumé tries to indicate the applicant's personality as well as goals, ambitions and attitude towards the job; an actor's résumé deals solely with work done, training and saleable skills. This makes for a special kind of résumé in both content and form.

Content

Your name is the most important piece of information on the résumé. It has pride of place at the top of the page. If you have an agent, you may be using agency stationery. This is a potential problem. Understandably, the agency wants its name to be displayed properly. On the other hand, you are advertising you, not your agency, and you don't want your name to be lost. Talk to your agent about this; you ought to be able to come to some sort of an agreement. Perhaps you could agree to have two résumé formats: one for the agency to send out and one for your own use (see Chapter Nine, "The Ten Percent Solution").

Do not head the page with "RÉSUMÉ." What else could it possibly be? A bowl of borscht? Don't waste the line.

You must display your permanent phone number. It is essential that a potential engager know where to contact you. All media casting and most theatre casting is done by phone. If you are using your agent's letterhead, the agency phone number and address is your contact (although you may also want to include your own phone number). If you are using your own paper, then your permanent phone number is vital. You can include your address as well, but most people will contact you by phone.

Your vital statistics come next: height, weight, hair colour, eye colour. Some casting people suggest that you have your age, or at least your age range as part of your physical description. We think this limits your casting potential. The moment you say how old you are, that is how old you will look: it is a self-fulfilling prophecy. If you let them make the decision on the basis of your photograph, without being influenced by seeing a number on a résumé, you will find that your casting opportunities will increase. So, no date of birth, no age and no age range or "playing age." As for the rest, do not lie. Or at least don't use a lie you can't get away with. If you plan to add a couple of inches to your height, you had better wear heels or lifts to all your auditions. If you insist on taking ten pounds off your weight (so much easier on a résumé than in real life) make sure your clothes reflect a slim image. (Better still, go on a diet.)

Actor's union membership must be put in. If you are not a member, it is not necessary to say "non-union." People will assume that if there is no information, there is no membership. Social Insurance Number, citizenship and marital status should not be included.

The main information on your résumé is your experience – professional, drama school, community theatre, student film. Engagers want to see what you have performed, to get an idea of your style and who you have worked with. When you compose your first résumé, this section may look a little skimpy. When we get to the section on **Form**, we will discuss how to show off what little you have to the best advantage.

Training next – not just college courses but workshops and classes. And not just theatre classes; include any in performance skills – dance, stage combat, singing, musical instruments, juggling, etc.

The last section is special skills. These are any abilities that increase your casting potential. Any sport at which you are proficient, any musical instrument you can play, any vehicle you can drive, any language you can speak, any accent you can use – this is the place to put it down. Do not put in hobbies unless they are professionally useful. Most engagers aren't all that interested in how well-rounded a human being you are. You aren't going to be around long enough for that to matter. We have seen résumés listing "reading" as a hobby. We assume that you read. Don't waste space that could be better used for wind-surfing or playing the guitar.

"Commercials on request" is an effective short form which demonstrates *on-camera* or *on-air* experience. It is not necessary to list the commercials you have been in. No one outside the commercials field is interested and you will have to list your on-air and up-coming commercials at every commercial audition you attend.

As your résumé fills up with professional and then union work experience, you will drop your college and non-professional *credits*. Next to go is the institutional part of your professional training. This means that you will delete your drama school training but will leave in the Singing Master Class with Luciano Pavarotti or the Television Presenter Workshop with David Suzuki. However, all that is in the future. For now, it is more a question of finding things to put in a résumé rather than deciding what to take out.

Form

Your résumé must be only one page. Trust us, more than one page will not be read. To be honest, even one page often isn't read. When you have garnered a huge number of credits, you will be selecting and distilling to keep it all on one page. Two pages is not twice as impressive as one – it is twice as much bother to read.

Without question, a résumé must be typed. Not only that, it must be typed on a good typewriter. If you do not own a decent typewriter or have a friend with one, there are other alternatives. Most universities have machines which you can rent cheaply by the hour; some public libraries and photocopy shops have the same service. If you are still at school, before you lay out any money, try the office typewriters. If you are on good terms with the office staff, you might get to use a machine. As a poor third, there are also typing services. These are far more expensive than renting a typewriter for an hour or two and you are at the mercy of someone else's interpretation of your layout.

As the authors drag themselves painfully into the twentieth century, they have to admit that résumés may also be typed on word processors and stored on floppy disks. If you have a word processor, setting up and storing the information is child's play. (Hah!) Once the résumé is stored, changing and updating the information is quickly done. If you don't have a word processor, you can buy a floppy disk and take it to a computer rental outfit. You then compose your résumé, take the floppy disk away with you and return whenever it needs changing, updating or printing. There are résumé services which will set up a résumé and store it for you, allowing you a couple of free updates for the initial fee. After that, you pay for each update. Beware – the résumé service that will compose a non-standard résumé is the exception.

It used to be that résumés were typed only on white paper. Then people started using coloured paper. The theory was your résumé would stand out from all the white ones. Now it is the white ones that tend to stand out as coloured paper becomes more popular. In fact, as long as the paper is reasonably heavy, it does not matter what you use. Our advice would be to go with something that looks classy and professional – fluorescent green doesn't.

By now you have amassed all the information for your résumé. Check your spelling. Make sure you have the correct title of the play or film. This is particularly important with films, whose titles can change between shooting and distribution. (One of the authors paid for a hundred copies of a résumé with the film *Twins* as one of the media credits. Three days later the title was changed to *Dead Ringers*. Result: a hundred useless résumés.) Decide what is going in. You are probably thinking that at this stage in your career everything should go in, if only to fill up the space. Not so. Empty space is better than second-rate credits. For example, unless you won some sort of prize at a festival, try not to put in any high school productions. There is no need, unless the résumé is very thin, to mention each individual teacher who has given you instruction. You will get most benefit from the names of those who are currently active in the business. At the beginning of your career, your résumé will be heavy on training and light on experience. Don't unbalance it more than you have to.

Your name, at the top, should be in larger and bolder type than anything else on the page. Assuming that you are doing your résumé yourself, without the help of a computer, word processor or professional printing, you can still set up your name effectively. Using Letraset or its equivalent is time-consuming but the results are excellent. Another method is photocopier enlargement of typing. The results are not quite so good but still acceptable.

The sections of a résumé are usually in the following order: personal information (contact address and telephone number, vital statistics, union affiliations), work experience, training, special skills.

Work experience is usually broken into stage and media work, under headings like Theatre Highlights, Selected Stage, Some Film Roles, Television.

Don't include dates in your work experience. By doing without them, you have removed any evidence of unemployment. Everyone knows that actors have periods when they are not working, but why call attention to them? It is far more impressive to list your most important credit first. (What makes it most important is up to you. It could be the lead role, or a famous director, or a prestigious theatre, or a prize-winning film – or just the first part where you had more than eight lines.) Remember that few people will bother to read the whole résumé. They start by reading the first few lines, then skim down to the end of the section. Capture their attention by starting with something eye-catching rather than your latest credit, unless your latest is also your most impressive.

Another possibility is to order your credits geographically. It can be useful for a director to know where you have worked, particularly if you can show that you have been to places more than once. (It is always reassuring for a director to see that you have actually been asked back somewhere.)

Professional credits, no matter how small, come before community theatre, student films and college credits, no matter how large.

Accentuate the positive. Don't panic because your work experience consists solely of school scene study and final-year products. Include a section called Workshops and list the scene work you have done. This is not cheating. You are making it clear that you were not taking part in fully-finished productions and you are giving the potential engager a picture of the kinds of roles you are familiar with and have worked on. If you have done one radio show, one television show and one film, having three separate sections is going to look rather bare. Amalgamate the three under Selected Media Work and present a more positive picture.

The training section may be arranged chronologically and if you want to put in graduating dates, that's fine. It can be useful to know how long you have been out in the real world and to see how much you have done in that time. Obviously, you will not put the dates in if you graduated two years ago and have done two days on a film since. The rule is: If it makes you look good, put it in. If it doesn't, leave it out.

In the special skills section, try to keep your skills compartmentalized. It is easier to get a picture of your accomplishments if they are not all strung out on the same line. For example, you can have a line for sports, another for dancing and singing, one for any musical instruments you can play, a line for accents or languages and one for any vehicles you can drive. Be specific. It is far more convincing to read "swimming (bronze medallion, life saving)" than just "swimming." Special Skills is also the place to put in your singing range and style.

Most actors' résumés have their credits arranged in columns. It is the easiest, clearest and most accessible way to communicate the information. Your layout need not follow our example as long as it is simple, neat and easy to read. Set adequate margins, try to keep the space between topics the same size, make sure all the columns line up. Accentuate section headings in some way (upper case, bold, underline, all three). Be consistent. If you decide to use both underlining and colons for the topic headings, make sure you use them for all.

Do not abbreviate anything unless you are sure it is common enough for everyone to recognize. The University of British Columbia is generally known as UBC, but it is unlikely that anyone other than alumni would recognize GBC as George Brown College. If the full title is threatening to ruin your beautiful layout, you can abbreviate it, type in an asterisk and put the name in full as a footnote.

Accentuate the names of the productions (under Selected Theatre and Selected Media) in some way, e.g., bold or upper-case. In the second column, avoid saying "various parts." Use either the biggest role or, if they are all of a size, the two most successful (Dotty/Liz) or the most interesting combination (Priest/Madman).

If it was a school production done outside the school in a "real" theatre, put the name of the theatre. If the production was for television, use the series title. Use the programme title only if it is a

EDITH EGGAR

Height: 5'5"
Weight: 118 lbs
Eyes: Blue
Hair: Dark Brown

192 32nd Street
Vancouver, B.C.
V9Z 1H8
(604) 555-7856

SELECTED THEATRE

Our Town	Emily	Carpet Theatre	Joe Lowe
The Pyjama Game	Poopsie	Nesbit Hall	Susan Carr
The Miracle Worker	Helen Keller	Webb Theatre	Ray Davey
The Crucible	Ann Putnam	U. of Vancouver	Lloyd Snow
Caucasian Chalk Circle	Girl Tractorist/ Ludovica	U. of Vancouver	Elise Jacobs

SELECTED MEDIA

E.N.G.	Actor	Alliance	Stephen Gold
Extension Courses	Principal	U of V Studios	Dan Frond
Banxx Rock Videos	Principal	Skeezit Prodns	Joanie Nolan
Stub it Out	Actor	Smokenders	Dan Zaley

TRAINING

BFA: University of Vancouver
  Voice: Nana Jory, David Greenberg
  Singing: Vittorio Silva
  Movement and Dance: Clarence Duthie, Peter Epp
  Stage Combat: Robert Bienfait

SPECIAL SKILLS

U of V gymnastics team, horse-riding (Western and English)
Singing (Rap, Rock, Classical Mezzo)
Driving (standard)

one-time special (series *E.N.G.* but special *Dieppe*). "Alliance" (in the third column) is an example of a **production company**; if it is a student film, say so.

It is better at your stage to use "Actor" or "Principal" (see Chapter Six, "Be Prepared") rather than the name of the role in media credits.

Proofread! Believe us, there is nothing more frustrating than receiving your beautifully photocopied résumés, all 150 of them, and then noticing that you played Ratty in "Toad of Toad Hell." Go through each section word by word; go through each word letter by letter. Yes, it is tedious. Yes, it is time-consuming. But yes, it is worth it.

Now you have your master résumé. How many copies to make depends on the number of people you plan to send it to right now and how often you expect to update it. Price per copy goes down with large orders but you won't save anything by getting a big stock that will be out of date before it is used up. Photocopy companies vary in their machines and their care. Unless you use a first rate one, all your hard work will have been for nothing. Photocopying, done on a good machine, will turn your master, with all its cutting, pasting and whiting out, into endless perfect "originals."

PHOTOGRAPHS

Don't waste money on fancy framing, tricksy shots, composites showing you in various poses, or colour film. There is only one publicity photograph actors need – the **glossy, head shot**, or eight-by-ten. Ten inches high and eight inches wide, stapled to the back of your résumé, taken by a specialist, a black and white picture of your face. Sounds easy? Wrong!

There is not a person in the world who is totally satisfied with the face that peers out of the mirror. We know how tempting it is to choose the most flattering or the most glamorous shot but it is a temptation you must resist. Your photograph should look like you on a good day, but look like you it must. It is a waste of your money and the engager's time to send out pictures which make you look like Brooke Shields or Tom Cruise if, when you walk into the office, you look like Olive Oyl or Hagar the Horrible. Sell what you are, not what you want to be.

With that warning in mind, be careful with your make-up. That goes for males as well as females. You do not want to look any more made-up in your photo than you do in real life. Making up for a photo session can be difficult. Many photographers have make-up artists who work with them. These people are experts in knowing how make-up translates onto a print. You must not allow the photographer to touch up the eight-by-ten unless the offending blemish is temporary. The mole on the cheek stays; the pimple on the end of the nose goes.

You may need more than one style of picture to send out. The photograph you use for commercial casting will likely be different from the ones you use for theatre or film. Each target has its own specifications. A moody, sullen shot, very effective for a specific role, might not be the ideal photograph to send to a theatre, which needs to see the closest thing to the "real" you. Photographs for commercials show high energy and lots of teeth. Whatever photographs you decide to use, make sure they have a good, strong image. There is little point in sending out pleasant-looking bland pictures of you which show nothing of your personality. You might as well send in your high school graduation picture.

The photograph should be a close-up. Although the current fashion among photographers is for a wider frame, we believe anything showing you below the collar bone is just waste space.

Most people take off their glasses for photographs. That's fine, as long as you do not wear them for interviews or work. It might be worth getting the photographer to shoot a couple of you with glasses on. You don't have to choose them but they may turn out to be surprisingly useful. In commercials, Paul Brown, an actor who lives in Toronto, made a name for himself with his elfin face and big horn-rimmed glasses. He was as instantly recognizable as the products he promoted.

The simpler the picture, the better. Beware of outdoor shots with a busy background. There is nothing wrong with having pictures taken outside – the light can be excellent – but foliage, brick walls or mountains can pull the attention away from that all-important subject. You. Please, nothing tricksy. A shot with your pet monkey might be momentarily diverting but think how embarrassing it would be if the monkey got the part.

Your focus in a photograph is vital. By that, we don't mean how fuzzy the picture is but where you are apparently focusing your attention. The more you seem to be looking at the person who is holding your eight-by-ten, the better. A clear, direct look is engaging and compelling; a sideways or off-centre glance is not.

Deciding which photographs to use is not easy. The photographer will supply you with one or two eight-by-ten contact sheets, usually with one roll of film (thirty-six shots) on each. Each shot is about one inch by one-and-a-half inches, and at first glance they all look the same – awful. You will want a magnifying glass of some sort, a good strong light and a couple of L-shaped pieces of paper so that you can see how a picture looks properly cropped.

You have two areas of decision, technical and professional. The technical side is easier to deal with. Is the photograph in focus? Is it too light? Too dark? Are you centred in the shot? Is your head cropped? You don't have to be an expert to make choices on the basis of these questions. Some problems – centering and overall exposure for instance – can easily be corrected for the full-size print. Where the technical problems are incurable – poor focus or dirty negatives – any decent photographers should agree to re-shoot free.)

Professional suitability is a more subjective area. You have to decide which photograph is going to sell you best. You need to think about image and energy and style: which picture shows the "real" you, which shot is useful for film and which is better for stage, what personality the picture projects. (If there are no useful shots, the photographer may agree to re-shoot for the cost of materials. He is arguably obliged to do so by law but it may come down to a battle of wills.)

Get as many outside opinions as you can stand. Certainly, you should ask the person who took the shots, although photographers tend to choose on the basis of what shows up their work best, not necessarily what is best for you. Ask friends in the business. Agents see hundreds of photographs and usually have a keen eye for what sells. They know their clients, how they come across in the flesh and which head shot best projects those qualities. If you are still in drama school, ask your teachers. (Be aware, though, that they may not have had any dealings with the professional side of the business for some years and may be out of touch.)

Whatever you do, don't ask your mother. She'll pick the one with the neatest hair.

Photographers

Choosing a photographer who is right for you isn't easy. Ask your agent, if you have one. Look at friends' glossies. The union offices have photographers' advertisements on their notice boards.

When you have a short list, call them and ask some questions:

- Do you produce actors' eight-by-tens? (If they only sell wedding portraits and graduation pictures, try someone else.)

- What is your session fee?
- How long is a session?
- How many shots do you take?
- How many eight-by-tens do you supply?
- Do you have a make-up artist?
- How long before the prints are ready?
- When is the first available appointment?

Compare the responses and ask for an appointment with your first choice just for a chat. Discuss your image, clothes and make-up. Ask to see examples of actors' head shots. How do you feel about the photographer as a person? Do you seem to have good rapport? Is this the sort of person you want to open yourself up to? Having your picture taken can be a tense and trying experience. If you do not feel comfortable with the photographer, chances are the session will not be successful. Discuss the method of payment. Any reasonable photographer should agree to part of the money in advance and the rest when you have satisfactory prints. This gives you some leverage if you are not satisfied with the results.

Repros
Over the course of a career, you will send out hundreds, thousands, of photographs. This would be prohibitively expensive if each one were an original print from the photographer or from a photo-finisher. You can now get cheap mass-reproduced prints in most cities, either from a photographer with the special equipment or from a specialist photo repro house. Photo reproducers make a negative from the print the photographer has given you and mass-reproduce it. (The original negative belongs to the photographer, not to you.) The cost of each print is no more than a fifth of the cost of a print from a photo-finisher. The photo repro service will add your name to the negative fairly cheaply. This is worth doing. It ensures that if your head shot gets separated from your résumé, it won't be an anonymous face impossible to file. Although they are called "glossies," head shots are now just as cheap in pearl finish, and just as acceptable. We prefer the look, just as we prefer no borders on the photo. If there isn't a repro house in your centre, Galbraith's and Graphic Artists (addresses on page 199) accept mail orders and send reproductions across Canada. It's worth a stamp to see how their mail order prices compare with the local competition.

Find out what people do in your area. In some cities actors can save money by using good photocopies or photo litho copies of their head shots, but check with your friendly local ACTRA office. You don't have to be a member. If you are sending your photograph outside your immediate area, only a first-rate photo reproduction, difficult to tell from an original, is acceptable.

You are not going to want too many repros done, once you have sent off your first round of photographs. The younger you are, the more quickly your look changes. You may find you need new photos taken before you next send out a batch. At any age, if you have cut your hair, gained ten pounds, developed wrinkles or made any other noticeable change to the way you look, you will need new glossies. As we said right at the beginning, your picture must look like you – the way you are now.

Demo Tapes

There is a third weapon to add to your promotional armoury: the demonstration or "demo" tape. It comes in two flavours: video and voice.

Video

A video cassette will show a selection of your media work. You will need some experience in film and television before you have enough varied and interesting material to put on tape. The tape is useful to introduce yourself to agents and casting directors who are unfamiliar with your work or who know you in only a limited context. In the past, agents often required actors to audition for them. Nowadays, if an agent hasn't seen you in action, the demo tape is a popular way for him to view your work. It doesn't necessitate his going to the theatre or the cinema. He doesn't even have to remember to switch on the television at a particular time to catch your little scene. All he has to do is put the cassette on at his leisure and there you are.

Getting tape of work you have done from the production company is not always easy and is sometimes expensive. Putting your best bits together on a demo tape is fairly easy if you are in a reasonably large city but it is very expensive – some hundreds of dollars.

When the authors asked a selection of casting directors how important they thought a demo tape was, the answer was a unanimous "very." But they did not agree on where that importance lay. Tina Gerussi: "It's a tool and it's very useful for my own purposes, when there's someone I'm not sure about and I want to reinforce him in my mind. But demo tapes don't really tell me what a person can do. They are simply an extension of showing your résumé, not necessarily showing me how good you are." On the other hand, Stuart Aikins: "The director uses the demo tapes to find out three things: (1) Can you act? (2) Are you directable? (3) Are you right for the role?"

Most of the casting directors feel that demo tapes are useful for audition purposes if you have a decent track record. Stuart Aikins: "I can't tell you how many times established actors lose stuff just because there's nothing to show a director if they are not available for the audition. Actors who are available for the shoot but can't make the audition should have a demo tape." But for inexperienced actors, Tina Gerussi: "For actors just starting out, using a demo tape instead of attending an audition (if you can't make it) is not all that great. The audition is all-important. Also, it depends what it's for. For episodic television, we don't look at a lot of tapes. There is a new show every ten days, casting sessions every few days. There are enough people around to choose from. If it's a big feature, you might just want to remind a director who a person is. But it depends on the material on the tape. If you've done a lot of work and have some juicy scenes to put on, then it's worth it. It won't get you a part but you'll get to meet the director. We don't show tapes unless there's something substantial to show."

The quality of the tape is something casting directors don't agree on. Brian Levy: "It has to be of excellent quality. Even if it's a good piece of work, if the production values are bad, don't use it." Other casting directors concur: "Don't put one together unless it is fabulous!" "Poor production values are the same as a lousy eight-by-ten – re-shoot it. If it is cheap and shoddy, people won't buy it." However, here is Stuart Aikins: "Slickness is always interesting but not totally necessary. As long as the material is visible and audible that's all that's important. I will even look at peer group tapes (groups of actors get together and work on scenes, rent a camera and record them). They can be useful, although I'd never show them to a director." Tina Gerussi makes a good point: "If you can get your demo professionally *edited*, do … Having the second ear and eye, that of the editor, helps to get rid of extra stuff you don't need or shouldn't have. It's an investment."

Your demo tape should be short. Brian Levy: "Actors make the mistake of having too much on a demo tape. Nine minutes is absolutely tops." Stuart Aikins: "Four minutes is best." Tina Gerussi: "Five to eight minutes. They don't get looked at more than that. Casting directors look at the tapes longer than engagers. Producers and directors look at a tape for about two and a half minutes. If something hasn't caught them by then, it's finished."

Most casting directors agreed that if you are *featured* in a film, you could put a long section on the tape after the short segments, for engagers who are interested in looking at more of your work.

Slating your tape is important. You must identify it at the beginning with your name and your face. For one thing, tapes can be put in the wrong boxes, and for another, if there are three young men in a scene, how is the director going to know which one is you? Tina Gerussi: "The worst thing is looking through a demo, not knowing who you're looking for." You can identify yourself in a variety of ways. First comes your name and your agency. Then a short (ten seconds) montage of close-ups. If that isn't possible, a ten-second viewing of your eight-by-ten, or a montage of eight-by-ten's, just to let them know what you look like.

Brian Levy: "Try to make the content of the tape as varied as possible. But remember, the people who watch it are likely to switch off after a couple of minutes. Start with something really effective." Stuart Aikins: "Segments should show a range – period, comedy, drama, action." All casting directors agree that you should put your strongest scene first, although some casting directors will cue up to what they think is your best scene before they let a director see the tape.

Having commercials on a tape is fine, as long as they don't overbalance the content. One casting director described a demo tape done as a television show: scene-commercial-scene-commercial, all done in about five minutes and very effective. Actors who do mainly commercials may want a tape showing only commercials, but for most actors there should be a proper balance of commercials and drama.

All casting directors said they vetted (and occasionally vetoed) the tapes before letting a producer or director see them.

Although many agents go to the theatre regularly, they are still interested in seeing demo tapes. Actors do not always come across the same way in media work as on the stage. No good agent wants to make a decision based on one type of show. Actors who can't reach a live audience may have the ability to bring an audience in to them on screen. Only a demo tape will reveal that.

If you do decide a videotape is worth its substantial cost, make more than one copy of the tape and never, never let the master tape out of your possession.

Voice tapes

Voice tapes are the audio equivalent of a photograph and résumé. The tapes are prepared by your agent and sent out to engagers who are looking for voices for radio and television commercials, documentaries or animation. If you are with an agency that does a lot of voice-over work, great. If not, you will probably find that area of the business closed to you. It is not something you can do without an agent, who has the facilities and the casting information you cannot get.

All right, you have all the equipment you need. Let's put it to work. Let's go to an audition.

Chapter Five
The Art of Auditioning

"Always behave like a duck – keep calm and unruffled
on the surface but paddle like the devil underneath."
– Jacob Braude

A ctors treat auditions as if their lives were on the line. Yes, you
should treat them seriously and professionally, but keep your
perspective. Marion Paige, New York casting director, quoted in
How to Act and Eat at the Same Time: "What's the worst thing that can
happen? You don't get the job. You didn't have it when you came in,
so what's the loss?" Treat the audition as an opportunity to meet
potential engagers and to sharpen your auditioning technique. If
you come out of the room satisfied that you gave the best showing
of yourself that you could, then the audition was a success. Getting
the part is a bonus!

With your photograph and résumé clutched in your trembling
grasp, you head for your audition. Whether it is your first audition
or your fiftieth, some things remain the same: the desire, the ner-
vousness and, most important, that photograph and résumé
clutched in your trembling grasp. It does not matter how many
times you have walked into the same casting director's office or
how many times you have auditioned for the same director, you
take a photograph and résumé to every audition. Stuart Aikins,
casting director: "I hate actors who don't bring photos and résumés.
It is self-centred and unprofessional." Tina Gerussi, casting director:
"I know a producer who won't hire actors, however wonderful the
audition, if they haven't brought their photograph and résumé. The
producer needs the reference. He's seen thirty people; how is he
going to remember who's who? Keep a set in your car, in your brief-
case. Make sure they're stapled together. And no excuses. 'I thought
my agent sent it,' is just dumb. We've heard every excuse in the
book."

As long as you are taking one photograph and résumé, take two.
You never know who else might be at the audition. If it is an audi-
tion for a musical, you can give the musical director the second set.
If there is an associate director present, it would be polite (and

unusual) to give your second set to him. An associate director today could be an artistic director tomorrow and will remember kindly those who remembered him.

Larry Lillo, Artistic Director Emeritus, Playhouse Theatre, Vancouver: "Make sure your picture looks like you. People walk in looking nothing like their pictures. It's a waste of time." Lloy Coutts, director and teacher: "Your photograph should look like you now and should show what sort of person you are."

Be on time – the first rule of any job interview. In this business, being on time means being early. Give yourself a chance to calm down, brush your hair and re-apply make-up if appropriate. Find out if any new information on the theatre is available. Look for brochures with the confirmed season. In media auditions, give yourself a chance to look at what you're going to have to read. Stuart Aikins: "You should look at the material in advance so that you can make choices ahead of time." Tina Gerussi: "For episodic television, the script gets in only just in time. Give yourself fifteen or twenty minutes with the *sides*." See if you can gauge the way things are being handled from the actors leaving the audition room. Chat to the people around you.

Sometimes you will be late; catastrophes do happen. Don't rush in breathlessly, tossing apologies to all and sundry. Apologize briefly to whoever had to juggle the schedules, then shut up. No one is interested in your traffic jam or stolen wallet. Don't apologize when you get into the auditioning room. The director may have no idea who is next in line until the actor appears. Why bring attention to your tardiness?

The audition starts the moment you walk into the room. You never get a second chance to make a first impression. How you greet the director and present yourself to the producer are as important as your prepared speech or reading. Larry Lillo: "When I was auditioning for Blanche [in *A Streetcar Named Desire*] I knew two minutes into the woman's audition that she was the one I wanted. It was something to do with the way she walked into the room, the way she said hello, everything." Edwin Stephenson, freelance theatre director: "I like a direct handshake and hello." Tina Gerussi: "The first impression is so important: how you walk into the room, how you present your photo and résumé. The handshake is vital. We know you're nervous, but cold, sweaty hands are not a good thing. Try to dry them off and warm them up!"

In fact, the audition really starts in the waiting room. There is often an engager's representative outside the auditioning room who comments on you before you ever get through the door. Be polite to everybody. The "receptionist" may be an associate director who popped out to use the phone. Ask which washroom you may use, where you may smoke, if you are allowed to use the phone. Don't knock the product before a commercial audition, don't make jokes about the theatre's personalities or political leanings. You are the guest in this situation, not the host.

Your physical appearance will affect the engager. Start from the skin and work out. Edwin Stephenson: "You should have bathed and your hair should be washed." Keith Digby, former director, Bastion Theatre, Victoria: "Everything is part of the audition. If you are dirty, I will assume you are careless about your work as well."

Dress appropriately. You want to feel comfortable and look attractive. You must be able to move the way the character you will play does. Don't wear anything that distracts from what they want to see – you. Lloy Coutts: "I feel cut off by heavy make-up, jangling jewellery, an elaborate hairdo." Michael Shamata, Artistic Director, Theatre New Brunswick: "Don't mask your shape with heavy sweaters or outsize jackets." Dress as you would for any other job interview. Actors' working clothes may be casual, even sloppy, but until you've got the job, dress so that your mother would be proud of you.

If you are auditioning for a specific role, you may dress with that in mind, but don't go in costume. You insult the intelligence and imagination of the engager. (On the other hand, if you are being considered for the part of a lumberjack, there is no point in wearing your Giorgio Armani suit.) The one exception to this rule is in commercials auditions, where the client may ask to see the actors in costume. We have seen actors turned away from commercials auditions for not complying with the costume requirements.

Be prepared. Jackie Maxwell, Artistic Director, Factory Theatre, Toronto: "I don't expect actors to know the specific plays in my season – most of them are new and unpublished – but I do expect the actors to have some knowledge of the theatre itself, the kind of work we do." Richard Ouzounian, former Artistic Director, M.T.C., Winnipeg; Neptune Theatre, Halifax: "You should do your homework; you should know the season and the previous *repertoire*." Larry Lillo: "If someone comes in saying, 'This is the part I want,' at least I know they've read the play. I expect them to know about the theatre. It's like any other job. If you go for an interview, you have to know something about the company. You don't go in and try to bluff your way through it." Bartley Bard,

Artistic Director, Lunchbox Theatre, Calgary: "I expect the interested actor to have a good idea of the type of material we usually do, what our audience make-up is and something about our operation in general. Otherwise, why are you contacting me for work?" Peter Mandia, Artistic Director, Aquarius Theatre, Hamilton: "Ignorance is not a big recommendation."

Preparation is important for media auditions, too. As a general preparation, ask your agent to show you different styles of sides for commercials. You should be watching television to find out what the market is. Tina Gerussi: "On episodic television, you rarely get told much about the story or character. You should watch the show before you go so you know the style, know what they're looking for. Nothing is worse on a regular series than an actor saying, 'What's the show about?'"

Although you may be informed in the morning that you have an audition that afternoon, there are still ways to prepare. Get your agent to read you the story synopsis to give you the best idea of the character. Make sure your agent tells you who is casting. Often there are two different auditions going on at the same place. Tina Gerussi: "For a feature film, try to find out about the director, if possible. Maybe something about his past work." Stuart Aikins: "I always give out sides the day before. Actors have no excuse not to be prepared." At the audition, read the copy again, make sure it's the piece you've been looking at, look for key words and, for a commercial audition, make sure you're pronouncing the product name right. The casting director will let you know.

The more information you have, the more confident you will feel. Confidence and a genuine interest and enthusiasm are almost irresistible.

The director is not the enemy. He would like nothing better than for you to succeed. God knows you would make his job an awful lot easier if you were perfect for the role.

Don't try to second-guess the director. If he knows exactly what he wants and you fit the bill, wonderful. If you don't, tough luck. Much of the time, the director doesn't know exactly what he wants. If he doesn't, how can you? Edward Gilbert, freelance director: "Don't try to second-guess me. Give me a straight and direct response to this moment as you are experiencing it."

Be yourself: that's the hardest piece of advice to follow. Every engager, every casting director we spoke to said the same thing: We don't want to see a routine. Tina Gerussi: "Present yourself as honestly and directly as you can." Larry Lillo: "Show yourself. I want to get a sense of what you as a person might have to offer." Michael Shamata: "All you have to offer is yourself." Jackie Maxwell: "Show me who you are before you pretend to be someone else."

Although "being yourself" should be a snap (after all, you've been doing it most of your life), it's the toughest acting job you'll ever have to do. The situation is tense and unnatural. If you were really being yourself, you would plead for the job or babble on about how nervous you are or embarrass yourself in a dozen other socially unacceptable ways. The auditioners understand your terrors and take them into consideration. Jackie Maxwell: "I try to make the chat as non-threatening as possible."

Saying "be yourself" is the same as saying your photograph should look like you. You should be presenting the best you there is. In *The Color of Money*, Eddie (Paul Newman) says of Vincent (Tom Cruise): "He's got to learn to be himself – but on purpose." You should project a confidence and an ease. Respond to the other person, listen, contribute. Try to make the audition easy for the auditioner. Edwin Stephenson: "The auditioner is working hard, too. Allow him to see you at your best." Answer questions fully. Work out the likely questions ("What have you been doing lately?" "What children's theatre have you done?" "Did you enjoy touring New Brunswick?") and have some answers ready (preferably more than "Nothing," "None" and "No"). The audition is an opportunity to tell the engager how you think, react and feel. Jackie Maxwell: "The director is looking for someone she wants to work with, not just someone who is good."

Don't lie. Although you want to paint as good a picture of yourself as you can, you've got to be able to come up with the goods. One of the authors got a part in a mini-series where everybody had to ride. Never having seen a horse outside of the movies, he responded modestly, "Well, of course, I'm not an expert," when asked about his riding abilities. However, he knew there were six weeks between the audition and the first shooting date, which gave him time for hours of expensive lessons to learn which was the front end of the beast. Unfortunately, it's the exceptions you'll hear about; they make the more interesting stories. No one talks about the actor who lied about a skill, was found out and fired from the job. If you do lie about a skill, make sure you have turned that lie into the truth by the time you have to use it. Your failures will stick in the mind much longer than any successes.

Know when to leave. Trying to extend the interview beyond its natural length won't do you any good. Learn to read body language.

Judge when the interviewer is preparing to say goodbye and get there first. On the other hand, don't short-change yourself. Robert Rooney, freelance theatre director: "Concentrate on yourself. This is your time. Don't rush to help them get back on schedule."

You may be offered advice in an audition about your photo, résumé, appearance or acting. It may not be what you want to hear but it was offered as a gift so accept it graciously. Don't argue or justify yourself. You don't, of course, have to take it.

THEATRE

General Auditions

The general audition is used by artistic directors either to meet actors for the first time or to see actors they haven't seen in a few years. You will normally do one or two prepared, memorized speeches in a rehearsal room or an office, rarely in an actual theatre. All the auditioner can find out is if you can walk and talk at the same time. Edward Gilbert: "I want some basic knowledge of the human being. And I mean very basic: height, weight, age, vocal quality. A general audition is only the first step in the process and quite a small one. I want you to pique my curiosity, encourage me to explore further." Larry Lillo: "It is the beginning of a process. You are meeting someone you may cast two or three years down the line."

General auditions usually have two parts: the interview and the audition speech, familiarly known as your "party piece" or "piece." Some directors don't bother with the interview as such. You walk into the room, do your speech and walk out. Some directors feel the interview is as important as the speech and spend as much time on it as watching you act. Be ready to go with what the director has decided.

The Interview The director is giving you an opportunity to show what you are like. Be prepared to talk about anything that might come up. Most directors use your résumé as a jumping off point for a discussion, so you should have interesting or amusing anecdotes prepared. We're not saying the interview is a scripted performance, but if you know a fascinating story or have some particular insight into a character, why not talk about it? Thinking about possible questions ahead of time means you won't suddenly find your mind a blank when the auditioner asks you how you liked playing Laura.

Don't bad-mouth anybody. A common question is, "How did you like working with So-and-so?" What do you say? What do they want to hear? Are they So-and-so's lover? If your relationship with So-and-so was like Lizzie Borden's with her father, how do you turn it into a positive experience? Remember, this isn't a test. It's just an easy way (so they think) to get you talking. Try to go from the personal to the professional. "It was the first time I'd ever worked with So-and-so and I learned a lot." From there you can segue into something you're comfortable talking about. However honest and open directors say they want you to be, listening to you knife one of their fellow directors in the back will make them itch between the shoulder blades.

The Speech Choose a part which you could actually play. Auditions are not the time to "stretch." Show your strengths. Go with what you can do, not what you aspire to. Jackie Maxwell: "What's the point in showing me a forty-year-old Brit? I'll never cast you as one." Show that you have some understanding of yourself. Douglas Riske, the New Bastion Theatre: "The choice of speech tells me what an actor knows about himself and his ability, and where he stands in his own development."

Many directors these days want to see pieces that show you. Larry Lillo: "Pick something you relate to, you care about, you feel comfortable with." Make sure it's a speech you enjoy doing. Nothing is more attractive and entertaining than seeing someone having a good time doing a piece.

Choose a speech that shows you in a way the company can use. Why do something from *Titus Andronicus* if you're auditioning for the Singalong Musical Dinner Theatre? Stephen Heatley, former Artistic Director, Theatre Network, Edmonton: "Know your theatre and know what you're auditioning for."

Look for a Canadian audition speech. More and more theatre companies are doing Canadian plays. Some theatres do nothing but, and require one or two audition speeches from Canadian plays.

Choose material that shows an emotional, physical and vocal range. Brian Paisley, former producer of the Edmonton Fringe: "For me, an audition is a time for the actor to show everything he can do, including movement and musical skills."

Look for a speech that is happening now, not a "memory" speech. Plays take place in the present. You want a speech that allows you an immediacy in your emotions and desires.

Keep it short! Directors don't need time to make up their minds. Jackie Maxwell: "You can have a sense of someone very quickly." Two minutes is quite long enough for any speech and no one will be upset if it's shorter. Never go over your allotted time. Audition schedules are tight and ignoring the time strictures will endear you to no one.

The speech should stand on its own. Edwin Stephenson: "It should have a beginning, a middle, and an end." You need to set up the situation but that's it. If you are prefacing a two-minute speech with a twenty-second introduction, something is wrong.

Most directors appreciate hearing new or unusual speeches. Don't choose something second-rate just because no one knows it, but if you can find something good and different, use it. Robert Rooney: "Why does no one ever do one of Shakespeare's minor characters? They've got some great speeches." Your material doesn't have to be from plays. You can use poetry, short stories, diaries, novels.

Don't risk embarrassing the director. Speeches that are overtly sexual, for instance, may work well in the play but on their own they are an assault on the sensibilities of the auditioners. From *Back Stage*, January 1987: "After three days of listening to lengthy, graphic descriptions of cruelty to children and animals, agonizing diseases, excretory functions, sexual perversions, tortured deaths and hysterical outbursts of scatological venom, assault is just what it feels like." Or, as Jackie Maxwell so succinctly put it, "I don't like obscenities yelled at me."

Make 'em laugh! The auditioners will be spending most of the day watching pain and angst. Anything light and witty will come as welcome relief.

Contrasting speeches do not necessarily mean "one classical and one modern." Speeches can be contrasting in mood, emotion, vocal range, character, point of view, physicality, place. Two plays written five hundred years apart aren't necessarily different in anything other than their language.

Keep your audition material ready to use. Lloy Coutts: "Read a play a week, at a sitting. Wait for a speech to offer itself. Don't force it. You should have six speeches and a song." With this size of repertoire, you will be ready to audition at the drop of a hat.

Speeches to avoid, apart from the "memory" speeches we've mentioned: (1) speeches from the previous season, (2) speeches from the coming season, (3) the great classical speeches, (4) characters playing other people, and (5) presentational speeches, such as prologues.

Read the whole play. You cannot possibly develop a three-dimensional character without that knowledge, nor can you carry on a discussion if the director uses the play to hang the interview on.

The introduction of the speech is as important as the rest of the audition. It should be clear, concise, simple and direct. Tell the director what he must know to understand the context and get on with it.

Some directors advise actors to take their time to prepare before starting a piece, others suggest leaping in. We think that actors often dissipate their energy by doing a whole preparation routine. Do that outside and use the introduction as your springboard into the speech. Why not walk out of the acting area and start your speech with a definite entrance? That way, says Edwin Stephenson, "you present the speech with an extra energy."

Don't stick yourself in a chair or stand motionless for the whole speech. Moments of stillness are effective but only when seen in contrast to movement. Start with a grabber. Katinka Matson in *The Working Actor* recalls being stopped mid-speech: "When they stopped me, all I could think was, 'But I haven't got to the good part yet!' You have to get to the good part right away." Keith Digby: "Grab the director in the first fifteen seconds. Make him ask, 'What next?'"

Put your better speech first. Of course, you do them both brilliantly but chances are you are more comfortable with one. An audition is not the place to get the worst over with first.

Use the space you have available. Do the speech far enough away to be seen full-length. On a stage, be sure you are in light. Use the voice that fills the space.

Avoid using props. Generally you're better off without them but occasionally a single prop can make a clear, dramatic statement. We once saw an acting student walk into the room, shake hands, introduce the speech and suddenly pull out a gun from behind her. It was exciting, if rather bowel-loosening.

Don't rely on furniture. Rehearse your piece without any or with a simple hard chair, which you will find in almost any audition space. Never fiddle with furniture or use it to hide behind; you're just putting off committing yourself to the speech.

Actors often fix the auditioner with a steely glare and address their pieces to him, as if he were another character in the play. Don't. Directors react in various ways, from Douglas Riske – "I wouldn't touch an actor who used me in an audition" – to Edward Gilbert: "If it is appropriate to the speech, I don't mind if an actor uses me." At best, it's unlikely to do you any good and it's a risk you can avoid. If you really think it's necessary, every director we spoke to wanted to be asked beforehand.

Move from the first speech to the second without dropping your energy. Rehearse the two as a unit. You are less likely to be stopped if you give the impression that the second half will be (even) better than the first.

The auditioner may re-direct you. Respond as openly as you can; jump in with both feet, regardless of how dumb you may feel. The director simply wants to see how you "take direction," what you will be like to work with.

Don't be afraid to stop your speech if you got started on the wrong foot. Don't be like one of the authors, who got a terrible attack of nerves at the beginning of a speech from *The Beaux' Stratagem*. Her mouth dried, her upper lip caught on her teeth and she played the entire speech like a Restoration Bugs Bunny. Michael Shamata: "If you screw up early enough, start over." Robert Rooney: "At least that shows you know the difference between your good and your bad." Mind you, you can only stop once. And your second attempt should be noticeably better than your first.

Don't start by apologizing. If you have a fever of 102° and a nose plugged up from here to Cleveland, ignore it. If you apologize in advance, you are setting the stage for a sub-standard performance, whatever you give them. If you can't manage to be "on" for fifteen minutes at the most, stay home. Phone to cancel the audition and take plenty of fluids.

It's going to happen to you, we promise. One of these days you are going to forget your lines right in the middle of your speech. What do you do? If you have read the whole play and are firmly grounded in the character, you can probably paraphrase your way out of the situation. Even if the director realizes what you're doing, he could well be impressed with your quickness of mind and ability to carry on. If the worst happens and your brain has truly ceased to function, just stop. Don't look at the director or try to explain. Take your time to recover your concentration; then, after a brief apology, finish the speech with renewed energy and attack.

When you have finished, shut up. Don't make a face, don't apologize, don't explain. The ball is in the director's court. If you have really screwed up, leave the "Oh, God, I want to die" routine until you get home.

Very occasionally, you will be asked to read something from one of the plays in the season, cold, without preparation. Having read all of the season's plays will help. They're not expecting your best performance, so dive in and have some fun with it.

The general theatre audition is the only one you may crash.

Theatres assume that actors who couldn't get official appointments will show up in the hope that someone will cancel at the last minute or simply not appear. Often this is a way for non-Equity people to be seen. If you do crash an audition, be extra polite. You are there hoping for the generosity of the theatre company. When you arrive, give your name, résumé and photograph to whoever is organizing the audition. Crashing is usually done on a first come, first served basis. And if you are lucky enough to get seen, make sure you write a thank-you note the moment you get home.

A postscript to crashing: The reason crashing is successful is that people with official appointments don't turn up. If you are ill or discover you have a conflict and cancel in good time, that's fine. If you just don't bother going, that is appalling. Not only are you messing up the theatre's schedule, for which they will not remember you kindly, you are also preventing another actor from being scheduled an appointment time.

Readings

Readings are auditions for specific roles, where actors are asked to prepare a given scene. Directors rarely use readings to meet new actors. These auditions are for people the director knows in some way. He's worked with them before or has seen them in a general audition or in performance.

In readings, the interview will be minimal. You may have a bit of a chat about the play, in which case you should be able to contribute your own ideas, but you're more likely to plunge right into the reading.

Leap in at the deep end with a definite character and a definite point of view. The tentative reading, which tries to play safe, is simply boring.

When you study the scene, find a powerful, effective move. It will free you and energize the scene and show how you might tackle the physical side of the character. Don't amble about for the sake of it.

Don't rush! If you give in to all that adrenalin, you will find yourself out the door before drawing a second breath. Take the time to make every moment count.

In the States, theatres hire good actors to read for the auditions. In Canada you will more likely be reading with whoever happens to be there – the stage manager, the associate director, the caretaker. Some readers go through the scene with no expression at all; some think they are God's gift to the drama and give big, bad readings.

How do you handle the problem? Work with a friend, giving each other flat or just plain bad readings. In the actual audition, try to use whatever you are given as honestly as possible. The director isn't stupid. He will see that you are reacting to what you are getting from the other reader. Don't try to force your version through like an armoured car.

Be familiar with the scene but don't work at memorizing it. Even if you do know the scene by heart, hold onto your script. Without it, the director will expect a more developed performance than is possible at this stage.

You should be able to do the accent, if the role requires it. The only exception to that is a *cold reading*, where the director suddenly decides to hear you as another character or even in another play. In an audition where you know what you are reading ahead of time, you have to deliver the goods. (See also "Call-backs," page 67.)

Singing Auditions

Even if you consider singing an activity to be done naked, wet and alone, you may find yourself faced with the prospect of doing it clothed, dry and in public. If facing a firing squad would be easier, skip this section. If you want to broaden your opportunities for employment, read on.

Preparation There's that word again. Can't we just go in and wing it? Of course we can. And here's the reaction when we do. Bill Skolnik, composer and musical director: "Nothing makes me angrier than an unprepared actor or singer. I want nothing to do with them, no matter how good they've been. It shows a lack of discipline. If someone says to me, 'I just found out about the audition this morning,' that cuts no ice with me. A professional is prepared." Thanks, Bill.

Some general auditions require two pieces and a song. Some directors ask for a song out of the blue. Bill Skolnik again: "Always be prepared to sing at an audition. Take your 'audition kit,' including songs and a pitch pipe, everywhere." There may be no accompanist. There may be no piano. These conditions are not fair but they do exist.

Regular singing lessons are expensive but they're a must if you are serious about auditioning for musicals. Doug Kier, actor, musician, and musical director: "Get a music teacher versed in musical theatre, not opera. Find a teacher you're comfortable with." Music teachers advertise on Equity and ACTRA notice boards, and in the

Equity newsletter. Talk to friends who take lessons. Shop around. Most non-singers need to build up their self-confidence as much as their vocal chords and the right teacher will be able to help.

Your teacher will help you prepare material that suits your voice and range. Bill Skolnik: "You should have a stable of songs at the ready and keep that stable maintained. You should have about four or five songs of different styles and moods so that on a moment's notice, you can just walk in. Have a patter song, a ballad, a comic song, a semi-classical piece (for those Shakespeare plays)." Doug Kier: "Look through all the musicals; learn the different styles."

Tape yourself.

Our tame experts don't always agree about specifics. Doug Kier: "If you can, find out the specific range of the role (top and bottom notes)." Bill Skolnik: "It doesn't matter if you don't know what the exact range of the part is." We suggest that you find out the general range (lyric tenor, baritone with high extension) and prepare material of the same sort that makes you sound good. Our experts do agree on one thing. Doug Kier: "If a director wants you, they'll be willing to transpose up or down a note or two." Bill Skolnik: "If you don't have the top two notes, it won't stop you from being hired."

If the audition notice requires a specific range, they won't transpose for you. If you haven't got the high A, don't audition.

New musicals are a problem. Doug Kier: "Find out the style of the musical – Gay Nineties, Noel Coward, Rodgers and Hammerstein, Country and Western, Rock Opera – and suit the song to the style of the show. I don't mind actors phoning to find out what they can. Be as prepared as possible. It's better than wasting my time in the audition."

Nerves are particularly dangerous in musical auditions. It's pretty hard to hide the quaver of fear in a sustained note. Bill Skolnik: "Everyone is nervous. I try to make people as comfortable as possible. If it's too bad, stop in the first five seconds. Then do it right. You've got to show that it's just an aberration. Deep breathing helps, so does chewing gum. Bring something to keep you warm. Keeping yourself at a good body temperature helps. Wear something that makes you feel comfortable and good."

According to Doug Kier, dairy products produce phlegm and should be avoided before a singing audition. According to the doctors we asked, all foods produce that coated feeling for some time after eating.

Approach your song the way you would a straight audition piece. Doug Kier: "To begin with, forget the music. Look at the lyrics in the context of the show. Find out as much as you can about the character and how he grows, in the song and in the play. Even if you are only doing part of the song, be as familiar as you can with the full piece."

Choice of Material Bill Skolnik: "Find something that shows off diction and range – especially diction. You have to show that you can take something musical and still be understood. That is something an actor can do as well as a singer, if not better." Doug Kier: "Singing is sustained talking."

Try to find a song that has not been done to death. Doug Kier: "There are songs from very famous shows that are not famous themselves. Also, are you Barbra Streisand? Judy Garland? Julie Andrews? Liza Minelli? No? Then don't sing *People, Over the Rainbow, The Sound of Music, Cabaret*. Avoid songs that are identified with a particular singer; they invite comparisons."

Bill Skolnik: "It is possible to do a song they've never heard of, but that may focus too much attention on, 'Who wrote that?'" Doug Kier: "Even if your wonderful Uncle Harry wrote this 'lovely song' – don't do it."

If one of the audition requirements is to do a song from the show, you do it. If they don't ask for anything, you must decide if you want to sing something from the show or do something that demonstrates you can handle the style, the range and the energy of the character. Mr. Skolnik thinks you should do something from the show; Mr. Kier doesn't, although he suggests that you have something from the show up your sleeve so you could do it, if asked. You pays your money and you takes your choice.

Our resident panel disagrees on one more thing. Doug Kier: "It's better to stick to the repertoire. If it's not from a show, it's not musical theatre style." Bill Skolnik: "I can be knocked out by a piece of music even if it's not from a show. I want to be entertained." (Don't ask us.)

Pick a song you know you can do well. Doug Kier: "It is much better to succeed at a simple song than to try something too advanced and wind up singing like a hinge."

Keep it short. Sound familiar? Unless you are specifically asked to do a long, dramatic piece, less is more.

Presentation Present the song the same way you would present a speech. You are trying to show the same things: character and emotion through voice and movement. Doug Kier: "A song's progress is one of action and character. It is not just a beautiful sound; you have to act the words, keep the character."

Bill Skolnik: "You have to know your space. Don't sell the song to two thousand people; sell to the four or five people who are there. Don't play to just the casting people. Play to the stage manager, the assistant stage manager, everybody. There's sure no point in playing just to the MD. I've never met a musical director in my life who's got to cast a show. All they do is get to veto."

Selling the number is vital. Doug Kier: "The general rule is that directors hire actors who sing, not singers who act."

Accompanist Bring your own accompanist if you can afford it and if the auditioners allow it (check first). You will feel more comfortable with someone you know and have worked with. If you are auditioning for something huge, like *Les Misérables*, you will probably have to use their accompanist and lump it. But with most shows, your own accompanist will be fine. Bill Skolnik: "The MD often accompanies and that's lousy. I can't hear and I'm concentrating on reading the music. That's why it's better to bring your own accompanist." Doug Kier: "Auditions can be ruined by a so-called sight-reader who (a) is nothing of the kind and (b) doesn't know what the word 'follow' means."

Make the accompanist's life easier. Bill Skolnik: "Don't bring music where the accompanist has to muck around flipping pages back and forth. At the very least you should come in with a legitimate piece of music that shows you can sing and that can be played without a great deal of strain by anyone who sits down at the piano and calls himself an accompanist." Doug Kier: "If the material is in the wrong key, get someone to transpose it for you. Don't expect the accompanist to do it on the spot."

TELEVISION AND FILM

You are not likely to audition for union media work in Vancouver, Toronto or Montreal without an agent. Casting directors send **breakdowns** (details of the characters to be cast) to agents, who send back suggestions from their list of clients. Casting directors choose actors from the agents' suggestions for the director and sometimes the producer to see. Outside the three big cities, engagers contact actors directly or hire a *casting agency* to do so. Non-union media work is usually advertised locally or cast through personal contact, which leaves that area wide open.

For the most part, a film or television audition is similar to, but shorter than, a reading for a theatre. The authors have been in and out of an audition room in less time than it took you to read this sentence. Well, that is probably an exaggeration, but auditions lasting less than thirty seconds are not unknown. You go in, smile, present your résumé and photograph, shake hands, sit down, read a short scene, get up, smile, say "thank you" and you're out. Now, if the director is seeing that thirty times a day, exactly how do you impress him enough to choose you?

Don't even try. All you can do is present an interested, vigorous you. Offer a strong, honest character choice and make it as real as you can. After all, what do directors want to see? David Cronenberg, film director: "The audition is often the first time I've ever heard the dialogue spoken. So I'm looking for readings that will make it come to life. Someone who does a wonderful reading, quite different from anything you've expected, can convince you that *that* is a better way to go. That's always very exciting. I try to be completely neutral in my expectations." Gail Singer, film director: "I look for a concentration, an ability to focus on the moment. Even if you are not the right person for this role, you might be for something else."

Concentrate on the reading. David Cronenberg: "What I'm not looking for is a whole routine. I'm not looking for someone to establish a personal relationship with me. I've seen all the tricks and I don't want them. Of course you have a little chat, you say a few words but you're seeing forty people in a day. You just want to get on with it. I know how vulnerable an actor is in an audition. His response to that pressure lets you know how he might react under the pressure of filming. The more stable you can appear, the better."

Don't be afraid to ask questions. Gail Singer: "An actor should ask for everything she needs." Brian Levy, casting director: "Ask anything that will give you a good handle on the character. You might just get the tip you need." David Cronenberg: "Any questions to do with the actual reading are fine." Listen to what you are told about the character and build that into your reading.

Often the part is just a couple of lines. How do you make a "strong, honest character choice" with, "The doctor will see you now?" Stuart Aikins: "Sometimes characters are just generic – the Doctor, the Lawyer. They are functionaries who are used as suppliers of information or they get the actor from one place to another. The only thing you can play is 'I want to do my job' and make a choice as to *how* you do the job. When you're faced with that kind of character, sometimes a physicality will give it life, create something a little fuller."

If you feel that there are a couple of ways to approach the scene, how do you choose? Go with your first, instinctive choice. You can't second guess the director, so you might as well give him your natural response. "But," says Tina Gerussi, "you have to leave yourself open. If the director gives you a totally different tack, you have to be prepared to let go of your preconceptions and go for something else. Be flexible." If you really aren't sure which would be the most effective reading, ask. David Cronenberg: "It would be fine if you could articulate that there are two ways of doing this scene, A and B, and ask which is closer to what the director wants. If the director says 'I'd like to see both,' do both. If he says, 'No, A would kill the scene,' do B. Of course, if you're going to do a reading more than one way, you've got to be sure you do two discernibly different readings."

Think of a film or television audition as a close-up shot. Stuart Aikins: "You don't 'present' to the director. Relate strongly to the other person reading, create a moment of intimacy. Make the director come to you. It's what the camera does." This does not mean that your audition should lack energy. Tina Gerussi: "The hard thing is to try to stay contained in your performance but give it energy at the same time."

As always, effective movement will energize your reading, but on camera, you may not have that choice. Tina Gerussi: "If you are being put on tape, you don't have a lot of space to move around. It's a good thing to learn how to be physical but at the same time staying stationary!" (Good luck to you.)

If there is a camera, the casting choices will be made largely or entirely on what is seen when the tape is reviewed. Every second on tape should show the energized, focused you. You will start the reading by slating yourself, which is media talk for naming yourself and your agent. Give the camera a straightforward, "David Desperate, Ronald Rip-off Agency." Then take a second (no more) to get yourself together and go for it. As with introducing your piece in the general audition, use slating yourself as your preparation.

Once the audition is over, out you go. Don't outstay your welcome.

Don't ask the casting director how you did. Brian Levy: "I'm not too happy about agents or artists phoning to ask for feedback on an audition. Most of the time, I simply don't know. However, if it's something specific or if it means a lot, like a starring role, I don't mind too much."

Most directors feel that the casting process is where most of their work gets done. Brigitte Berman, film director: "Finding the right person for the part – that, to me, is the most terrifying part. You've got to get the right ingredients for the story, the right ingredients so the actors are good together, the right ingredients so that you can work with the person and that person can work with you."

And after all that, Stuart Aikins: "A director's choice is almost always arbitrary."

CBC Toronto used to hold general on-camera auditions for theatre school graduates but time and money restrictions have put a stop to that. However, they still bring people they've not seen before into the office for auditions. CBC TV Talent tries to see twenty to twenty-five new people on Wednesdays. They try to reserve places for actors without agents – four per Wednesday. Claire Hewitt, deputy head of talent, CBC TV: "Please check about the Wednesday sessions. We'd like to hold them regularly but we've not been able to. I have found them extremely useful and have certainly cast out of them. Not leads, of course, but smaller parts."

At the CBC in Vancouver there is a casting director but no general on-camera auditions.

COMMERCIALS

The routine for commercials auditions is pretty standard. You check with the casting director, who gives you a sheet to fill in. (Make sure you've brought a pencil.) Put down your name, age, height, weight, clothes sizes, agent's name and phone number, your ACTRA number (if any), if you are available on the planned shooting dates and – most important – any on-air or upcoming commercials. Clients are paranoid about a possible conflict. If you have done a commercial for IGA recently, the Safeway people won't want you doing one for them. Put down everything; your idea of a conflict and the client's may not be the same.

If you are already booked for one of the possible shooting dates, say so. You may lose the job to someone else no better than you because you aren't completely free but that's better than being cast and having to turn the job down. Casting directors don't like being let down and they have long memories.

Give the form to the casting director, who will then take your picture. Even though you should have brought your photograph and résumé, they will often only use the snapshot attached to the form. Give them a look as close to the character as you can.

Make sure you arrive in plenty of time to look at the copy. Brian Levy: "A commercial script can be broken down like any other. Approach it exactly the same way." Eugene Beck, director of commercials: "The actor has to be an instant study and make strong clear choices." Sometimes you are paired with another actor in the waiting room. If so, get together and work on the copy. If you can develop a strong character relationship, you are both ahead of the game.

You should be familiar enough with the script so that you can lift your eyes from the page and make contact with the other actor. Try to learn the cues and your first words so that the interaction can be seen. Memorize the last line of the copy so that you can "give eyes" at the end of the scene. There is no point in showing only the top of your head.

Sometimes you will be given the basic situation but no script. If you know that you will be improvising dialogue, try to work a few things out ahead of time but be open for the unexpected.

You will rarely go into the audition room on your own. Either you will be one of three or four people auditioning for the same part or you will be combined with the rest of the characters in the commercial.

In a taped audition the camera is your auditioner. When you slate yourself, do it with energy and a smile. Give your name, your agent's name and keep up your energy and focus into the camera until it passes on to the next actor. You will be judged on what the camera sees.

Just in case they are taping the audition, don't wear black or white. Even with the most modern cameras, medium shades photograph best.

What do directors want in a commercial audition? Eugene Beck: "Can you bring life to the part and make it believable? Most parts are unbelievable. Can you make something special happen to an unspecial situation?" Look for an odd quirk that makes you an individual.

Casting a commercial is a serious process. Eugene Beck: "What happens on the *floor* is the least of what directing is. The audition is harder than the day of shooting for the director, too. I have to find out the personality of the character. You get five good actors but only one or two will be right. You are matching a person with a given set of ideas."

You may be asked to do almost anything, from a major improvisation to simply showing the camera your forearms or eating a peanut with integrity.

You may find this degrading and you may be right. Eugene Beck: "Be prepared to be asked to do some awfully silly things. Be prepared to be embarrassed." If you are going to go to commercials auditions, you have to be serious, committed and positive. (It may help to think of the big cheque.) Eugene Beck: "It is up to the actor to present enthusiasm, interest, personality. There are actors who don't really want to do commercials and walk in with a chip on their shoulders, yet they want the work."

Think about commercials not only as good money but as media work in a concentrated form. Tina Gerussi: "When you're casting small parts in films, people don't get a lot of screen time to give out those two lines. It's a lot easier to do a scene that explains everything. Lots of actors think, 'Oh, it's just two lines; I can do that.' It doesn't work that way. Commercials train actors to get the message across very quickly. I watch for that. Commercials are valuable to do and valuable to see. That's what casting directors do when watching television, concentrate on the commercials!"

VOICE-OVERS

Nothing to it. If you've got the special skills and the voice(s), the audition is straightforward. You tape the copy at your agent's or the casting director's. You don't even have to change your clothes. Outside Montreal, Vancouver or Toronto, voice-over auditions are held at whatever studio will be doing the recording.

RADIO

The main body of radio drama (between 60 and 70 percent) comes out of CBC Toronto. Linda Grearson, the present casting director, sees actors on Mondays; call to ask for an appointment (see page 199). The audition consists of a chat and a reading. Also, Linda Grearson says: "I try to see as many plays as possible. If you're in a play, it's worthwhile sending me a notice in advance; I'll do my best to attend."

CBC producers across the country cast their own shows and like getting voice tapes. Beth Russell, former casting director, CBC Toronto, suggests: "Your voice tape is the general audition. The cassette tape can be prepared in your own home — whatever costs the least amount of money. Put together a tape of no more than four minutes in total, with an opening *monologue* that is contemporary, speaking in your own voice — very naturalistic. Then you can do one or two other monologues, whatever you wish. Do a piece with an accent if you feel you can handle the accent *very well*. Don't worry about performance quality as long as you slate the tape at the top, identify the speeches one by one, and record them at a level loud enough to be heard when it's played back. It doesn't have to have everything you are capable of doing; just an indication of acting ability and general vocal quality."

People who cast radio want to match a face to a voice. Always include a photograph with your résumé.

Edmonton is the only city we know that has more than one radio drama outlet. As well as the CBC there is ACCESS Radio, which has a casting director who screens tapes and recommends actors to producers.

CALL-BACKS

You've made it over the hurdle of the first audition. Now they want to see you again. "Why?" we hear you cry. There are several possibilities, none of which is a desire to make your life miserable:

- Not everyone with a vote was at the first casting session. Other people have to see you before a final decision is made. You have seen the director but not the producer. You have auditioned for the artistic director of the theatre but not for the person who is actually going to direct the play.
- The engager wants to make sure that there is a good balance between all the characters. You look fine by yourself but may look too old to be the lead's younger brother when you're standing next to him.
- They have seen twenty-two Biffs and have narrowed their choice down to three. They want to compare you more closely with your competition.

Do not try to impress them with a whole new approach. They asked you back because they liked what you did in the first place. If the part has an accent, your grasp of it should be much firmer at a call back. Otherwise, give them the same energy, commitment and enjoyment you gave them before.

Also, give them a chance to see you in the same clothes. Wearing basically the same outfit will help to identify you.

There will be a great deal more tension second (or third, or fourth) time around. The stakes are higher; everyone has more to lose. Try to accept it, then ignore it. Directors appreciate any actor who minimizes the stress.

You are paid for your second and subsequent call-backs on commercials auditions, unless you have been asked back to audition for another role.

SEX

Unfortunately, sexual harassment and the *casting couch* are alive and well. Equity and ACTRA, who frown on nudity and semi-nudity in auditions, have strictly enforced rules and we suggest you read the relevant Agreements. If the audition is for a non-union production, you have only self-preservation and your common sense to protect you. The union Agreements will provide you with a useful guideline. Occasionally, directors come in from out of town and hold auditions in their hotel suites. Nine times out of ten, the auditions are as straightforward as those held in church basements (no vicar-and-choirboy jokes, please). Just watch out for the tenth. If you feel you are being harassed, you probably are. The best thing to do is remove yourself from the situation quickly and calmly, making your lack of interest very clear. Stay calm when you inform the union. Don't rant and rave; save that for when you warn your friends. Don't bottle it up; you are a victim, not a villain. Blow the whistle, loud and clear.

REJECTION

You could tell they liked you, you felt good about what you did. Why didn't you get the part? David Cronenberg: "You can't second guess why you didn't get the part. There are so many things that don't have anything to do with you or your performance. It's just the chemistry of the movie or the style of acting I'm looking for. I know that someone is wrong to play opposite an actor I've already cast. I can know that the minute they walk into the room. No matter how good they might be, it just isn't going to work." It could be your appearance. One of the authors was once told that she was too short to be a mother! Eugene Beck: "You don't know the factors that weigh in getting the part. The client may want the woman to look the way he remembers his wife looking twenty years ago."

Don't take rejection personally. Eve Brandstein in *The Actor*: "Detach your identity from rejection ... You are a salesman selling your acting services and that's all there is to it." Don't let rejection affect your enthusiasm or drive. Easy to say, hard to do. Being rejected is a major part of most actors' lives but you never get to like it.

Nobody likes doing the rejecting, either. David Cronenberg: "I think about the other side, about rejection. I say to the casting director, 'Please let that person know that I thought he was really good, that I like his style but he's just wrong for this role.'" Not many directors go to that much trouble but nobody enjoys turning you down.

You will never stop auditioning, however powerful or successful you become. Auditions become less formal and eventually you will be offered jobs without auditioning for them first, but the audition process never really ends. Deal with each opportunity as a single step, another try, and one day soon you will be dealing with the hassles in the following chapter.

Chapter Six
Be Prepared

"Keep strong if possible. In any case, keep cool."
– B. H. Liddell-Hart

Your troubles are over. The audition was great and the phone is ringing with a job offer. Sorry, my friend, your troubles are just beginning. You are about to enter the big, bad world of negotiation. Let's freeze the phone in mid-ring and take some time out.

First, you have to decide whether you want to do the job at all. In the early stages of a career, almost any job in the business is better than no job. Any job will give you new contacts. Any job will add to the professional credits on your résumé. But what if the part calls for a nude scene? What if the product you are being asked to promote offends your political or social views? What if the film, in which you are to play a perfectly ordinary bank teller, is actually a soft porn flick? Decisions you make early in your career about the kind of work you are willing to do may affect you years down the line.

Hold on, something else before you pick up the phone. Make sure it *is* an offer, not an availability check. If you are asked whether you are free on Tuesday, April 9 or whether you have any commitments for the months of October and November, that is not a job offer. It is simply asking whether you are available for work on those days. An availability check may include talk of the programme or play, the role and the money but there is no commitment on either side. Many an actor has had a drink on the strength of an availability check only to wake up the next morning to deal with the double whammy of hangover and unemployment.

Don't touch that receiver! When they quote money, how do you know if it's reasonable?

FEE STRUCTURE

With some leeway for individual negotiation, your fee will be determined in union media work by the size and importance of your role and in union stage work by the size of the theatre. In non-union work, fees are lower and less structured but these union rates give you a ball-park figure.

Television and Film Categories

- **Principal:** a performer who speaks eleven lines or more of dialogue or who has a major role with little or no dialogue
- **Actor:** a performer who speaks ten lines or less of dialogue or whose part has individual characterization regardless of the absence of dialogue
- **Extra:** a performer who does not speak and has no individual characterization and who performs, either solely or in a group, activities that the ordinary person could do

These are rough-and-ready definitions, which change slightly depending on the specific Agreement but are good enough for our purposes. In terms of pay, Principal has the highest daily minimum: $375 to $425. For Actor it's $225 to $275, and for Extra it's $90 to $125. Both Principal and Actor get paid *residuals* for programmes that are used again but the Extra is paid on a one-shot basis.

Commercials Categories

- **Principal:** a performer with a speaking role
- **SOC:** silent on camera (but with individual characterization)
- **Extra:** basically just a warm body to fill the background

Usually, there is more money to be made per day in commercials than in film and television work. The daily rate is higher and *use fees* can amount to as much as twice the original fee every thirteen weeks. However, unless you are a star or identified with a product (the Glad Man), that money is non-negotiable. The daily session fee (for your work in the studio) is the same for Principal and SOC (close to $500) but the Principal gets a higher use fee for the broadcast. Extras are paid only a session fee (around $200), no use fee.

Radio Drama Categories

- **Principal:** an actor engaged to perform a major role
- **Actor:** a performer who says ninety-nine words or less

Principals get paid more than Actors, which makes radio drama the only occasion on which you may legitimately count your words – get out those calculators, boys and girls. The fee structure is based on the length of the programme and whether it is going to be aired locally, regionally or nationally. Half a day in the studio brings in about $100 to $200.

Theatre Categories

Theatre categories range from A to G and are based on the theatre's potential box office receipts. The larger the possible revenue, the higher the minimum fee to the actors. Naturally, you may negotiate above that fee but the theatre may not pay below it. At the time of writing, the fees range from around $600 a week (minimum for an "A" house) down to $365 a week (minimum for a "G" house). On tour, you get around an extra $85 daily expense allowance to cover out-of-town costs. The Small Scale Theatre Addendum and the Co-op Agreement offer different pay structures and conditions to help more experimental work.

We are talking about union theatres' fees to union actors. Outside the union, it's anybody's game.

We know you're getting antsy but the phone is still frozen and this is a major point.

NEGOTIATION

Negotiation is an expression of the balance of needs between artist and engager. You have something they want; they have something you want. Negotiation is the process by which the two sides come to an agreement on what they will give to and take from the other.

We have all had the feeling of wanting to pay someone for the privilege of letting us work. We have to remember that we have something they want. They are getting as much from you as you are from them. They are not offering you the job out of the goodness of their hearts or because they feel sorry for you. They want you! If you enter into a negotiation knowing it is a two-way street, you are more likely to get your points across.

Working as a media extra, you don't negotiate, you get scale, the union's minimum fee for the size of the role. Theoretically, all other contracts are negotiable, even at the start of a career. In practice, a beginning actor doesn't have much clout and certainly media contracts are impossible for the neophyte to negotiate. A fact: two-thirds of ACTRA members work for scale. Not until you are playing major roles or are much more experienced in media work will you be able to negotiate effectively. Therefore, the following section relates mainly to theatre work.

Whether or not you have an agent, in theatre the original offer is likely to come to you. So pick up the phone.

Rule #1: *Never say "yes" immediately.* (Quote from an actor character in a deodorant ad: "Three rules of Hollywood: *never* answer the phone on the first ring, *never* say 'I'll be right over,' *never* let them see you sweat.")

No engager should expect an immediate answer. Your job is to get as much information as you can during the first call (role, dates, money, etc.), thank them for their interest, express your interest and say you will get back to them.

Rule #2: Put the phone down and yell and shriek with joy.

Rule #3: Once you are calm again, assess your situation. In most cases, you will not be given all the time in the world to make your decisions. Engagers are eager to get casting tied up as quickly as possible. Without committing yourself, you can express an interest in the offer and ask for time to think about it. You must be prepared to be pressured; engagers excel in this game of nerves. And you must be prepared to lose. It is possible for an engager to withdraw an offer at any time if you do not decide quickly enough. We are not suggesting that you delay making a commitment just to prove you are not desperate for work but if you truly have doubts don't feel obliged to give an immediate reply. Things are seldom as urgent as they are painted.

If you do have an agent, now is the time to get in touch. Your agent will negotiate for you, but it is up to you to set the limits of the negotiation. After all, your agent works for you and should not be making decisions that are yours to make. Since you should know every step of a negotiation let's assume you're handling things yourself.

Even if the offer comes from the director, you will be negotiating with the business manager. First, do your homework. Find out as much as you can about the company. Talk to actors who have worked for it. Find out the union minimum for the job. In the breathing space you have given yourself, work out what you would like and what you really need. Make up your mind in advance where you would draw the line and refuse to sign the contract. (We know that the last sounds unlikely but it does happen.)

Suppose the theatre offers you $365 a week. You find out from fellow actors that the theatre often pays $400 to inexperienced actors. Armed with that knowledge, you can make a counter-offer of $425 or $450, which gives the theatre space to counter your counter. (Yes, it would be easier if they simply offered you the $400 in the first place and saved all this hassle but why should they? After all, you may have been dumb enough to accept their first offer. God knows, we used to.) Decide ahead of time whether you will settle for their first offer if you try to get more money and fail. If the money is non-negotiable, perhaps the theatre could help out with accommodation. Maybe they would agree to some form of *billing*. They might say yes to a full-price economy air fare instead of an advance booking rate. Even a poor non-union film production company may give you a free *dub* (a copy of your scenes), to use in a demo-tape later on.

Rule #4: *Practise*. Make a list of Things to Talk About. Use a friend to role-play. Improvise phone calls. Some people find it easier discussing face to face, being able to study the other person's body language. If you are one of them, you will have to hone your telephone skills until you are comfortable communicating that way. You may rather enjoy using the phone. It allows you to have all your points written down and no one can tell that you are actually working from a script! Practise being devil's advocate. Making up arguments for the engager means there will be fewer surprises when it comes to the real thing.

Rule #5: You won't get everything you want. In the beginning, you might not get anything you want. Don't let that stop you trying. If you don't ask, you certainly won't get.

Rule #6: *Get it in writing*. A verbal agreement is legally binding if you have agreed on the following:

- Role
- Dates (beginning and end of contract)
- Location
- Money

But taking a dispute to court is a lengthy and expensive business, to be avoided at all costs. So cover a verbal agreement with a follow-up letter giving the essential details agreed on and an invitation to correct any misapprehensions. The letter should contain:

- Name of the artist
- Name of the production company
- Role
- Name of the production
- Date of first rehearsal and final performance
- Money
- City in which you will be rehearsing and performing
- The wording of any special details you want in a rider (see page 77)

This letter is particularly important when dealing with a non-union company. If the engager is in good standing with Canadian Actors' Equity, an Equity contract should be available. If the contract is delayed, you should send the letter. But check with the Equity office first.

This may seem like tedious and unnecessary drudgery but it's a lot more fun than arriving at the first rehearsal to find someone else reading "your" part. Oh, yes, it does happen.

Rule #7: Negotiation is serious but it's not war. There is no need to treat management as the enemy. They want to get your services for the least amount of money and you would like to work for them for as much money as possible. Within those boundaries there is a variety of options to be explored and discussed. Whatever you do, avoid confrontation. Go into negotiation feeling that you and the engager are working together to find a solution that is acceptable to both sides. That way, everybody wins.

After you have been in the business for a few years, you will become more demanding. Although you should have developed more confidence and a knowledge of where you are in the bargaining hierarchy, don't be afraid occasionally to accept a lower-than-usual offer. Brian Levy, casting director: "Don't restrict your work possibilities by insisting on doing only principal roles. If you do well in an actor role, directors have long memories." We can vouch for the truth of that. One of the authors was asked to audition for a tiny actor role in the pilot TV Movie of the Week, *Cagney and Lacey*. She hadn't worked in a while and decided to go for it. After auditioning for the three-word part, she was on her way out the door when the director called her back and asked her to read for another role. She got it. A two-handed scene – her and Loretta Swit. (Don't you just love happy endings?) Brian Levy continues: "That also applies to your fee. If you 'only work for double scale' [twice the minimum fee] for commercials, you may find you are cutting off a portion of potential work. You can always hike the fee up again." If the advertising agency has budgeted a particular part at scale to scale-and-a-half, you won't even be considered if your agent and the casting director know you "won't work for that kind of money."

Don't be too grand to work as an extra. We know established principal actors who work as extras on commercials. The money is useful, the work is easy and, who knows, you might get upgraded.

THE CONTRACT

A contract is the written record of a verbal agreement. If you sign it, you are agreeing to all the provisions as written down. So, *read it first*. If your agent signs your contracts, you should arrange to be told ahead of time exactly what they say. If the contract is for film, television or radio, you probably won't even see it until the day of filming or recording. It will be shoved under your nose, a pen will be thrust into your hand and you will be told to sign. Don't be pressured into signing before you have gone over it thoroughly, despite the sighs of impatience and toe-tapping from whoever is handling the paperwork. Take the time to check every section: dates, part, money, and riders (if any).

The engager must sign the contract and initial all the changes and riders before you sign and initial. Otherwise you are committed without getting any commitment in return. Make sure, in an Equity contract, that you sign all four copies. Send Equity's copy to the office immediately; don't let the theatre send it. Always keep the original top copy of the contract.

A non-union contract needs careful reading. If you have been given a non-union media contract, your local ACTRA office may give you a copy of the appropriate union Agreement so that you can compare it with your contract. If they are not terribly busy, they may chat to you about possible problems. If you live in Toronto or Vancouver and have a non-union theatre contract, the business representative at the Equity offices may look at the contract and offer suggestions. Again, this is done on an ad hoc basis and only if the rep has the time and the inclination. You could have a lawyer look over the contract. Although seeing a lawyer can be expensive, it could save you future costlier problems. In Toronto and Ottawa, there is an excellent service: ALAS (Artists' Legal Advice Service) has lawyers who give free advice on arts-related problems. If you live anywhere in southern Ontario, it would be well worth the bus trip to take advantage of this organization. (See page 199 for the phone number.) Unfortunately, there is no similar service in the rest of Canada. Unless you have a tame lawyer in your family, or know someone just coming out of law school who might want to practise on you, your cheap choices are limited.

A theatre may ask you to sign an "as cast" contract. This means that the engager wants you but is unable or unwilling to tell you what your role is to be. It may be that the director is casting you for an entire season but hasn't finished the specific casting for each play. It could be that a play you are to do is still being written and no one, including the playwright, is sure what characters are going to remain in the script. Whatever the reason, you are being asked to sign a contract with no assurance of the role(s) you will eventually be playing. Your decision to accept or not will have to be based on the reputation of the theatre and director, and on your need for the pay cheque. "As cast" contracts are not necessarily bad things, especially at the beginning of your career.

A signed contract before you start work is your only legal protection. Union engagers are obliged to have you sign before you start and union actors are forbidden to start without having signed. Usually, you will receive a theatre contract well in advance, which gives you plenty of time to remedy any errors or omissions. Media contracts often don't arrive until the first work break. If you start work without signing, you are tacitly agreeing to all the provisions in the contract and are legally bound by them. However kind and reasonable the management, why open the door to possible disputes? All it takes is a few minutes to read the contract, make sure it is in order and sign it. A five-minute wait at the beginning of work could save several days' arguments and many long-distance phone calls.

On media jobs, at the end of the day you will be asked to sign a time sheet, which is a record of your hours worked and breaks. You will sometimes be asked to sign a blank time-sheet before the work has been done, not from any evil motive on the part of the management but simply because it makes the production assistant's life easier. CBC Radio Drama is notorious for doing this. All around you, actors older, more experienced and theoretically wiser are signing blank sheets. The pressure for you to do the same and not to make waves is enormous. Try to resist; it's like asking you to sign a blank contract. Engagers don't often make mistakes and will pay off when overtime is due, but be aware that if anything goes wrong, you have signed away your power to fight. (The authors sign the time sheet and add in brackets, "signed blank." Or enter the time it was signed.) If you are working as an Extra, you will be given an Extra voucher at the start of the day's work but it will be filled in and signed when the work is done.

RIDERS

A rider is a special provision added to a standard contract. Riders must be mutually agreed on in discussion before they are written into the contract. You should not be expected to sign a rider you have not discussed. More times than we care to remember we have received contracts with great lists of riders added by management, none of which had been discussed ahead of time. Often they are harmless, unremarkable and unnecessary and all you can reasonably do is sigh inwardly and sign. But other riders are not so harmless, unremarkable and unnecessary and they must be dealt with before signing. The easiest way to avoid problems is to ask the business manager during negotiation if the theatre has any riders it wishes to add. (Something to add to your list of Things to Talk About.)

Anything can be added as a rider to the contract if both parties agree and, in the case of a union contract, if Equity allows. If you want the theatre to provide baby-sitting services for your child and it agrees, put it in the contract. If your agreement includes the theatre's paying for your accommodation, put it in the contract. If the theatre is sincere about these extra provisions, it shouldn't mind adding them as a rider. If the theatre assures you that it agrees and that there is no need to insist on these riders – beware! If these people don't want to put their signature where their mouth is, chances are they have no intention of fully honouring the agreement.

A rider's wording is crucial. Compare: "The theatre agrees to provide baby-sitting services for the artist's baby while the artist is in rehearsal or performance" with "The theatre agrees to provide baby-sitting services acceptable to the artist for the artist's baby at all times that the artist is engaged in theatre business, which includes but is not limited to performance and rehearsal calls, wig fittings, wardrobe calls, publicity interviews and photo calls." See the difference? The most crucial phrase in the second, improved version is "acceptable to the artist." This means that when you arrive at the theatre with your bundle of joy, you won't be greeted by the director's Aunt Lucy, ninety-three years old and wacko, who cheerfully admits that she loathes children but she's getting a free ticket to opening night for baby-sitting. Or, if you are so greeted, the theatre cannot say, "Well, you wanted a baby-sitter, there she is. We have fulfilled our contractual obligations." The clearer and more precise the wording of the rider is, the fewer chances there will be of misinterpretation or disappointment.

Does your name appear on the poster and in newspaper advertising? How large is it? Does it come first or last or somewhere in the middle? Above or below the title? Are you mentioned in publicity releases every time the play is mentioned? These questions and others are what a billing rider answers. At the beginning of your career the question of billing is likely to be academic – you aren't going to get it – but it becomes more important as the years go on. Even early on, it could be a bargaining point with a small, non-union theatre. The theatre may not be able to pay as much, so to sweeten the deal it agrees to give you some sort of billing. It costs the theatre nothing and makes you feel good.

Billing is a tangible sign of your worth to the production. (In many cases it is also a tangible sign of how tough your agent is.) Although some managements still shy away from it, billing is becoming more and more part of negotiating a contract.

JOB CONFLICTS

If you are offered a job and you want it, you may find you have a job conflict. It is a cliché in this business that either no one wants you or everyone does. Actors can go for months without a nibble, then be presented with three jobs at once. And, life being what it is, all three offers will be for the same time period.

What do you do? How do you decide which one to take? (Remember, no one can make these choices for you. Your agent and your friends in the business can advise and suggest but only you can decide.) What are the factors you have to weigh? In no particular order they include money, role, prestige of the theatre or film/TV company, location, director, length of contract and your gut reaction. You are rarely offered the perfect job so decide what your priorities are in each case. The play may be exciting but the money dreadful. You might want to work with a particular director but the part is not one you feel comfortable with. You may not care for the script but it means doing a scene with Robert DeNiro. The pay is great but the show is touring northern Manitoba in February. One job is a brilliant showcase for you, the other job will get you out of debt. One show is a pilot for a possible series, the other show is a secure ten-week contract. Just to complicate matters further, there will come a time in your career when the type of role you play will determine your decision. If you have been offered your sixth pathological killer, do you say yes knowing you will be successful, or do you opt for something new and challenging at which you might fail? All these questions boil down to: "How will this job affect my career?"

All you can do is find out as much as you can about the offers, take a good, hard look at your present artistic, professional and financial situation, and get advice and suggestions from people whose opinions you respect. And don't forget your gut. Sometimes an immediate instinctive reaction is as good a barometer as anything.

You are going to make wrong decisions. It is inevitable. Comfort yourself with the knowledge that some of the greatest learning experiences come from bad choices, and besides, you get far more entertaining stories out of disasters than successes!

RESEARCH

Once your theatre contract is signed and sent you may think you have nothing to do until your first day of rehearsal. Wrong again. Try to find out as much as you can about your working conditions, the people and the place. Talk to people who have worked with the director or at the theatre or just in the city. If you know other people in the cast, great. Chances are you won't know many. Again, see if you can discover something about them. This isn't crucial – after all, you will find out soon enough if you are going to love them or hate them – but it can be comforting just to have a basis for a conversation at the first coffee break. Very little of this will be possible for media jobs but you might ask around about the director's way of working or see one of the television programmes he has directed.

A theatre bringing in actors from out of town often provides an information pack about the city: restaurants, cinemas, laundromats, public library, main post office, bus routes, city maps, etc. It usually contains specific theatre information as well: theatre doctor, dentist, chiropractor, bank and lots of company rules and regulations. All this information is vital but you won't get it until your first day of rehearsal. If you get into town a day or two ahead of time, it would be comforting to know where to find your nearest supermarket, drug store, liquor vendor and other services necessary to life and ease. Before you leave home, go to your public library and look at a street map of the relevant city, if only to get some idea of where the digs the theatre is suggesting are in relation to the theatre.

Going out of town demands planning ahead. We know what *we* do – a finely-balanced routine based on running around in frenzied circles – but we thought the following might be useful. We are grateful for tips from a friend in her excellent book, *See the U.S.A. with Your Résumé*, published by Samuel French.

Are you going to sublet your apartment? Make sure you've got notices up in laundromats, the union offices, your agent's office and neighbourhood supermarkets describing the place and the dates available. Tell your friends to keep their eyes and ears open. If you find someone (preferably through a mutual friend), put the sublet agreement in writing: beginning and end dates, who pays for what, instructions about pets and plants, no sub-sub-letting, fuse box details, phone bill arrangements.

Arrange for mail forwarding. Type up a stack of labels with the theatre address and buy some big manila envelopes. Get your flat mate or sub-let (ask nicely and supply stamps) to shove your mail in an envelope every so often. It's cheaper and sometimes more reliable than the Post Office's mail-forwarding service. Stop the forwarding ten days before you're due back.

If you are planning to drive to your job and it's out of province, find out what the provincial laws are concerning car insurance. Some provinces assume that if you are living in their fair land for longer than thirty days, you have become a resident and must re-register your car.

Make sure your provincial health care insurance is aware that it is receiving bills from some nasty foreign province because you are temporarily resident there. Otherwise, they may decide after some time that you have changed your base and will just stop your coverage. Drop off a note to your province-of-residence, assuring them that your heart is true and faithful and you will be coming home. Otherwise, you could find yourself uninsured in both provinces.

If you are on any sort of medication, tell your doctor how long you will be away so that you can stock up on enough pills and potions. Take your optical prescription. Carry these (along with your script and any necessary theatre information) on the plane with you. Be safe – carry a change of clothes and a face cloth, too: luggage gets lost.

Find out ahead of time, if possible, how well your accommodation is equipped. In any case, take the following items: sharp knife, can and bottle openers, corkscrew, rubber spatula, non-stick frying pan, saucepan, coffee/tea maker(s), salt and pepper, herbs and spices, and a couple of J-Cloths. (You won't be able to take your entire kitchen and bathroom with you, so your first shopping trip will probably include paper towels, detergent, cleanser, toilet paper, Kleenex, soap, laundry detergent and light bulbs, as well as your food staples.)

You will also want an alarm clock, a radio or cassette player, extension cord (the lights are never where you want them), bath towel and washcloth, hair dryer (for home or the theatre), vitamins and aspirin.

However busy you are going to be, don't lose contact with the outside world. Remember to take your address book, writing paper, envelopes and stamps, pictures and résumés, stapler and staples, scissors (for office or kitchen), calendar or diary, scratch pad, pencils and pens, Scotch tape, needles and thread.

Will you be ready for the weather? In this country, unless you are performing in Tuktoyaktuk, where the temperature is a pretty constant -40°, you should take at least two seasons' worth of clothes, a bathing suit (there's always the Y if the ice is still on the lake), rehearsal and work-out gear, and at least one reasonably grownup outfit.

The item you are most likely to forget? Your alarm clock. Don't ask us why.

Take enough cash (the first week is always the most expensive) to see you through until your first payday. You should be able to get an advance from the theatre if you run short but it's a hassle. This is where a credit card can save your life.

And you thought you were going to have nothing to do. Most important, the time between signing the contract and starting work is the perfect time to research the play and the part, particularly if it is a period piece. Phillip Silver, designer: "As a designer, you spend a lot of time researching the way people look, the way they behave, the way in which they move ... Often you find that the ... actor himself hasn't done the leg work. You design a lovely pile of costumes, put them on the actors and (a) the costumes don't look right and (b) the atmosphere of the world you're trying to create historically doesn't look right, because nobody's bothered to look at a John Singer Sargent painting to see how ladies held their hands in 1885. I would like to see actors spend more time on understanding the world out of which the plays they're working on come. Look at pictures, listen to music. Actors think that just to read the script, to be able to say the words, to breathe properly and to do interesting movement is enough. It's not. There is a whole world you are trying to create." Kate Greenway, stage manager: "Think about what you can bring to a project. If it's a period piece, outside your own experience, do some research. I am amazed at the number of people who don't. It's important not only for your individual character but for the general ambience."

Once you have received the script from the theatre (try to get them to send it with the contract), you have the opportunity to read and re-read without any pressure. Take advantage of it. You will soon be caught up in the rehearsal process, where unpressured time is rarer and more precious than rubies.

Chapter Seven
Heigh Ho, Heigh Ho

"A mystique has grown up around acting …
but [the stage] is where you do your job and find the
satisfactions that come with doing well the job you like."
– Claire Bloom

THEATRE

The Nightmare: You arrive at the rehearsal hall for your first day of work. In your concern for punctuality, you have arrived half an hour early. The door is locked, it's February in Regina and the nearest coffee shop is in Saskatoon. Time passes. You finally walk in. Who are all these people? The play has five people in it; there must be forty-five in the room. Why does no one else look nervous? Where is the director? You're bound to recognize him. But will he recognize you? Someone shoves a cup of coffee in your hand, tells you she is Publicity and they need that hundred-word bio ASAP (*"What?"*) You all troop over to the model of the set with the designer. You are right at the back of the crowd and can't even see where she is pointing. She passes around the costume designs. You love what's she's done for all the characters except yours. Suddenly, the room is emptied of all but a few and the director is giving a little speech about the play. You double check your script. Yes, he seems to be talking about the same piece; why don't you recognize it? It is time to read the play. You listen desperately to the other actors, with one trembling finger holding the place in the script where you first appear. They are all wonderful! They Are Getting Laughs! What am I doing here? … Wait a minute. He's not so great. Hey, I could do better than that. Why didn't *I* get that part? Oh, no! I'm next. Here goes … Oh, God, I want to die. That was terrible!

Enough! What seems to be a nightmare is actually a typical first day of rehearsal. It's overwhelming; it's challenging. It's terrifying; it's thrilling. You're at the top of the hill, ready to ski down. It's scary but it's also as exhilarating as hell.

First Day

Quite often, you will not be rehearsing in the theatre building. Stage management should inform you of this ahead of time but it is probably just as well to check. Lauren Snell, production director: "Make sure stage management can get hold of you. The stage manager has her own anxieties. If you are not going to be at the contact number the theatre has for you, make sure your agent knows where you are." When you speak to the stage manager or ASM (assistant stage manager), she should tell you how far the rehearsal hall is from your digs and how to get there. If she doesn't tell you, ask. If she doesn't know, she will get back to you. It's part of her job to see that you have that kind of information.

Many theatres get their whole work force – secretarial staff, technical crew, publicity, *Wardrobe*, designers, actors – together for the first morning with a "Meet and Greet." Some of these people you will never see again in your five- to ten-week stay. Some you will see far too often. Usually, there are doughnuts and coffee, everyone is introduced and the *general manager* or artistic director makes a little speech of welcome. You then mix and mingle and try not to look as terrified as you feel. Remember, you're not the only one suffering. Not only are the other actors nervous, however well they hide it, the stage manager is nervous, the director is nervous. They have responsibilities you have not even considered. Introduce yourself to as many people as you can. Try to meet the head of Wardrobe and the designer. If the stage manager is doing her job, she will make herself known to you. If not, find her. Don't be afraid to admit you are nervous. Kate Greenway, stage manager: "Everyone is nervous. You are not alone. Relax, smile, don't look like it's the end of the world. Horrible things rarely happen so early."

Some directors encourage the support staff to stay through the designer's show and tell, the director's chat and the read-through. Other directors clear the room immediately after coffee and doughnuts. Whatever the decision, the actors' preferences are not considered.

The designer will describe his work: the functions of the set, scene changes and costume designs. Evan Ayotte, designer: "The designer's main sources of information (like the actor's) are the script, which he has read over and over, and his discussions with the director." Phillip Silver, designer: "The difficulty between the designer and the actor lies in the fact that the director and the designer get together very early on and make basic decisions about the show." They have to. Budgeting, drawing and some fabric buying have to be done before rehearsals start. Designs are made before the parts are cast; designs are made with certain actors in mind, who turn out not to be in the show. Directors describe actors in one way and in reality they look quite different. Evan Ayotte: "It is quite a rude awakening for designers sitting in the first read-through, seeing the collection of people they are going to have to execute designs on."

The director's little talk – and not all directors give them – can be about anything from the way he plans to approach the play, to why he chose it, to the value of teamwork. Don't worry if you find yourself disagreeing with his "vision." Those concepts can change during the rehearsal process as the director becomes influenced by what he is getting from the actors. Whatever he says, it will give you an insight into the person who, for the next few weeks, will have more effect on your life than anyone else.

The read-through is full of stress. Remember, you already have the job; you don't have to impress anyone with how good you are. This is not a final performance, just a chance for everyone to hear how the whole play sounds before it is taken apart and worked on piece by piece. It is tempting to judge other actors' work by a first reading and to assume they are doing the same with you. Don't. It is a waste of energy. Just get on with reading the play as honestly as you can.

If this is an Equity (union) theatre, union members will elect an Equity deputy. The deputy's job is to act as liaison between the theatre management and Equity. The deputy works with the stage manager to avoid potential problems, ensures that the theatre pays all overtime and travel expenses, and much more. Only union members may elect the deputy and all non-union members must leave the room while the election takes place.

The stage manager, also known as the SM, will hand out infor-mation packs. These will contain an assortment of goodies such as maps of the city, lists of restaurants, drug stores, cinemas, banks, supermarkets, liquor stores and interesting sights and activities. You will probably get scene breakdowns and a proposed rehearsal schedule as well as a performance schedule. Kate Greenway: "Even if you don't ever read it, please don't leave it behind! It's an insult to the SM who has spent much time and effort compiling all the information." The SM will also discuss company business such as rehearsal times, meal breaks, the day off and pay day. (You have to be paid by the evening before the final banking day of the week.) Usually the theatre has asked you, by letter or in the first phone call, to bring your publicity material. This is the time to hand it over to the SM. Lauren Snell: "With things like your bio and photo please bring them if asked. Other people have severe deadlines." This is the "hundred-word bio ASAP" from the nightmare. Every theatre publicist has a programme deadline in two days and needs a brief blurb to put by your name. They may offer to whip something up from your résumé. Don't let them. They'll only put things in you want left out and leave things out you want put in. Do it yourself.

You will probably get your measurements taken later in the day. Often the theatre sends you a chart ahead of time which asks you to measure everything you can reach and many things you can reach only with the aid of an intimate friend and a step-ladder. Please do it. After you have filled it out and handed it over, you will find that Wardrobe wants to do it all over again. (Don't ask.)

When all the business is completed, you will finally get down to the real reason for the next few weeks – rehearsing the play.

Rehearsals

We are talking here about mainstream Equity theatres. In other theatres, the process is the same but the hours of work stretch and the breaks tend to be forgotten.

A rehearsal day is usually seven hours out of eight or eight and a half (depending on the length of the lunch break). Rehearsals can be as short as ten days in summer theatres to four weeks in some of the larger provincial theatres. (The two large festival theatres, Stratford and Shaw, have quite a different set-up. You can rehearse for months, since several plays are rehearsed during the same period.)

Some directors begin by having the cast read the play several times, with discussions between read-throughs about character and relationships. Others begin by blocking the play, getting the actors up on their feet right away. Even the process of blocking may vary from one director to another. Some have very clear and specific ideas of where they want the actors to move; others know the broad shape of the action in terms of entrances and exits but let the actors "feel their way" around the acting area before making any decisions of exactly where they should go. The stage manager writes down all the blocking as it develops. Lauren Snell: "Write down your own blocking, it's a help. It means the stage manager doesn't have to split concentration and coax an actor over to the right side of the room by waggling her head towards the general target area."

Although in theory the theatre may have you at rehearsal all day long, in practice you are usually called only for those hours the director will be working on the scenes you are in. Mind you, very few directors manage to keep to their schedules, however hard they try, so be prepared to do some waiting.

The rehearsals will be broken up by costume fittings, wig fittings and possibly publicity sessions. Evan Ayotte: "Ideally, you should have two costume fittings. The first is a silhouette fitting, just for shape and fit. The second is for the details and balancing elements. The actor should come to the fitting prepared to gesture and move in character. The actor should realize that a good designer is there to give the actor's ideas about the character a visual reference, as much as the director's ideas. The actor should consider the fitting and talk with the designer as a further extension of the rehearsal period."

With few exceptions, rehearsals are closed to anyone other than cast and stage management. This allows you to experiment, and if necessary make a fool of yourself, in private. Toward the end of rehearsals, you may have people dropping in. They are not there to watch a performance as such but are concerned with the technical aspects of the production – lighting, sound, quick changes of set and costume. Each new person who comes in raises the anxiety level by one notch.

By the end of each day's rehearsal, the director and stage manager will have worked out a schedule for the next day. It is up to the actor to get that information; it is not up to the SM to give it to the actor. Lauren Snell: "Any stage manager worth her salt will feel paranoid if she hasn't given the actor the call herself but it's not always possible. The director might not give the call until 5:55 and you've been released at 3:00. It's a help if you call stage management. Even better, when you leave at 3:00, let the stage management know you'll be calling just after 6:00."

To begin with, you will be working with rehearsal props and furniture, with the scenery marked on the floor in tape. Kate Greenway: "Pay attention to the lines on the floor. The stage management has spent forever lining them up." When you start rehearsing, you will probably not want to work with any props, since one hand will be holding the script and the other will be holding a pencil and turning the pages. As you learn the lines and start to come *off book*, a good stage management will have rehearsal props for you to work with. Be aware that all the clever business you invented is going to disintegrate once you start using three-dimensional objects. It is amazing how difficult it is to set a table with real plates and cutlery – and how noisy. The next step can be even more painful. Going from a mimed gun to a material gun is hard. Going from a rehearsal gun whose shape, weight and balance you have got used to, to the performance gun whose properties are totally different, is a nightmare. Be patient with yourself. All these transitions are a natural part of the process. No one expects you to get it right the first time. Which is just as well.

As rehearsals go on, the physical moves become more important. This is the time when accidents happen, before the routines are set and while adrenalin is up. Fights and dances are obvious times when you are physically at risk, and part of the choreographer's and fight director's job is to be aware of this. Accidents often happen, though, in ordinary rehearsals as new things are added. Kate Greenway, "Problems sometimes come up late and actors have to adjust. No one should do anything he or she considers dangerous." One of us fell headlong down a flight of stairs wearing costume shoes that didn't have dance rubber on the soles yet. Don't let enthusiasm make you careless.

Line learning is an individual process; there is no right way. Many actors learn their lines in rehearsal, so that the lines and the blocking are absorbed as a unit. During the day, when people are not actually rehearsing, you will see groups of actors running lines. There are actors who hate doing that and find that being alone at home, with the script or a tape recorder, is the best way to learn. A drawback of the tape recorder is the time it takes to record everyone else's speeches in the scenes you are in. However, it does mean that you are independent of the other actors when you wish to study. Some directors give deadlines for line learning. Whatever you think of this idea (and one of the authors doesn't think much of it), you will have to abide by it. Be prepared to have forgotten every single line the first time you lay down your script. We wish we had a dime for every time we've heard someone (ourselves included) say, "But I knew it on the bus!"

Be prepared for another shock when you run the whole play for the first time off book. This process is called, with good reason, a *"stumble-through."* To say that it will be an unmitigated disaster is to be kind. Most of your energies will be taken up with, "Which scene comes after this?" and, "Is this the exit we changed yesterday?" and "God, this is going fast. Did we leave anything out?" Don't let the shambles upset you. It is part of the natural process and within a week you will wonder what all the fuss was about. Work out a consistent routine for prompting with the SM. Let her know if you want her to call out the line or to let you struggle with it. Lauren Snell: "I sit there and see an actor with a wonderful strangulated look. Is he saying, 'Don't give it to me; I'm really trying to learn it' or, 'What's the matter with you? Why aren't you giving it to me?' Trouble is, it's the same look. Let me know ahead of time. And whatever you use – 'Line,' 'Please,' 'Yes' – be consistent."

Another transition to overcome is moving from the rehearsal room to the stage. Suddenly, you seem to have less space between pieces of furniture, there are stairs where there used to be a flat surface, the acoustics of the space are different. In the rehearsal room, there was eighteen inches between the end of the acting area and the wall. Now you have hundreds of feet to the back of the auditorium. Everything is on a slightly different angle. The sight-lines dictate your entering from ten feet farther back so that all the timing has changed. And on and on. Don't panic. Be patient with yourself. This, too, will become familiar and easier to work with.

Tech Week

As opening night approaches, you may feel that the actors are becoming less and less important to the production. They are. We are entering the world of the techie. Don't worry, the actors come into their own again but for now, rehearsals serve the technician. Remember, most of them have little or no idea about the play. Now they rehearse their work and learn the rhythms of the production. Now they discover how the set and costumes work, how well the designers foresaw the actors' problems when they made their drawings.

Tech week needs patience, patience and more patience. It is a time to hang on to what you've discovered in rehearsal. The best thing you can do is keep out of the hair of the techies and stage manager. Look what has to happen between the close of one show and the first tech of the next:

- The last show's set is *struck* and carted away to storage or to the dumpster.
- All the furniture, *props* and *set dressing* are sorted, returned to lenders, stored or trashed.
- Costumes are dry-cleaned, mended, sent back to the rental house or stored.
- Much of the lighting is struck; most of the colour *gels* are stored.
- The new set is assembled on stage and the basic lighting is hung and aimed.
- At least some of the furniture is put in place, supplemented with old friends from the rehearsal room.

About now, the actors arrive, all perky after a day off and eager to get on. The crew has been working with minimal breaks since curtain down on the last show and look what they still have to do:

- Hang the rest of the lights, re-*patch* the board, focus and fit the gels. Put together the sound *FX* tapes and place the speakers. Finish painting the set.
- Hang the doors, build offstage stairs and platforms, carpet offstage walkways, set up masking *flats* and *backdrops*.
- Rig practical lamps, fireplace *effects*, rain, explosions.
- Fix door knobs, locks and catches, light switches.
- Connect telephone, radio, stove, refrigerator, sink.

Tech week, or production week, may in fact be as short as thirty-six hours and then a technical work-through, a dress rehearsal and opening night. This is not the time for an actor to bring up any artistic problems. Try to have solved, or at least shelved, all artistic questions before now. During this time, everyone is tired, overworked, nervous and self-absorbed. Tempers are short. The best thing you can do is be available and keep out of the way – read a book, do a crossword, play cards, talk about how good you think everyone is, look at your script. What you do not do is complain about things outside your control.

These days are long as well as hard, running as long as twelve hours (much more if it is a non-Equity company). You may arrive at noon and not get near the stage until 4:00 p.m., although you have been on call all that time. When there is a break for coffee or lunch, take the opportunity to get out of the theatre. A change of venue can freshen you up.

You often start with a cue-to-cue (or Q to Q) rehearsal. Instead of your going through the whole play, the SM will ask you to start a few lines before a technical cue – the hall light going on, the sound of an approaching car – and then carry on until the SM tells you to stop. (If you have a quick costume change and the SM doesn't mention it, don't be afraid to ask for time to practise it before the Q to Q. Sometimes, because of time constraints, the Q to Q is the only technical rehearsal you have before the tech dress, where you will not be able to stop when things go wrong.) Q to Q's often turn into tech work-throughs, where you do the whole play but expect to be stopped when there is a technical problem.

The tech *run-through* is where the techies learn how long they have between cues, so don't stop unless the set falls down. Try to keep a mental note of any problems while you are on stage and the moment you exit write them down. Otherwise you won't remember until you reach the same point in the next run-through. Nine times out of ten the SM will have noticed it anyway but there is always that tenth time. Pass on the information to the stage manager at the note session.

The technical dress rehearsal, or tech dress, is the first time all the elements of the production come together. Although some directors don't mind if you do the tech dress without make-up, it can be useful to wear it, particularly if it is a heavy character make-up or if you are wearing a wig. Before the tech dress there is occasionally a formal costume parade, where you all troop out in costume to be seen by the director and designer. Often the director dispenses with a formal costume parade and uses the tech dress to observe and make notes on wigs, make-up and costumes. These notes he discusses with the designer, who is making her own far better and more detailed notes, and then with the actor.

A dress rehearsal, in the Canadian Theatre Agreement, is defined as "a rehearsal where the full company has been called in costume and make-up for a run-through." If there is an invited audience of the theatre's and the company's friends and relations, it is called an "invited dress." If the general public is admitted, paying or not, it is called a "public dress" and counts as the first public performance.

Previews
Previews are designed to help actors and director judge the audience response to a play. They are a particularly useful barometer for comedies. You will be able to find out more precisely where the laughs are in a show and where you will have to wait for audible reactions. (It is amazing how often cast and director can misjudge where a big laugh comes. Things that had everyone rolling about on the floor in rehearsal do not raise a titter in performance and those lines which you all felt should be cut, end up by bringing the house down. The preview is the place to discover all this.)

Theoretically, everyone has less riding on a preview. It is made clear to the audience, by the fact that the tickets are cheaper, that they are not getting as finely-tuned a production as they would see later in the run. Actors are assured, "It's just a preview. Use it." However, no matter how clearly we know on one level that a preview is just another chance to clean up and fine-tune and discover, we still treat previews as though they were "real" performances. Your first preview is, in effect, your First Night without the cards and presents. There you are with lights, costume, sets, props and a real live audience. What actor could treat it like just another rehearsal? Your body certainly treats it like the real thing, with surges of adrenalin to help you fight this dragon of a play.

The director is likely to give notes after the previews. After all, they are still part of the discovery process. Quite often the notes incorporate what he has learned from the audience reaction to the work. Although there still may be some rehearsals until opening night, and after, what you are performing during the previews is basically what you will be performing for the whole run. (There are some exceptions to this, particularly with new plays and musicals, which can alter drastically from preview to performance, as the writer uses the information gleaned from the audience responses to re-shape the work.)

Some theatres, because of time and budgetary restrictions, do not have previews. In that case you are thrown right from your final dress rehearsal into your ...

Opening Night

It's here! The night you have all been waiting for. The goal to which all your concentration and energy – emotional, psychological and physical – have been directed. Even if you have had a week of previews, there is still something special about openings. Maybe it's the knowledge that tonight the critics are in the house. Maybe it's the sight of the First Night cards and bottles of wine. Maybe it's the fact that you are throwing up in the toilet. Whatever it is and however it affects you, there is no denying that opening nights are unique. There is a buzz of excitement and energy that you feel at no other time. It is a remarkable natural high that can be as addictive as any controlled substance.

The Run

You've done it once. Now do it again. And again. And again. Keeping a performance fresh, clean and alive is the mark of the professional. It is easy to give a sterling performance when the adrenalin is coursing through your veins and everyone is high on the First Night. Try doing a similar performance three weeks later at a matinee, when the house is only a quarter full, three cast members have the flu – and you're one of them – two people aren't speaking and you have to do it again tonight. Try doing it three weeks into the tour, after riding in the van all day. Try doing it on a stage that won't quite hold all the set. It is your responsibility to perform, as closely as you can manage, the play as rehearsed. We are not saying that the show shouldn't change. Of course it should – and will. But those changes should come out of delving more deeply into the text, discovering nuances in the playing and exploring avenues there was only time to touch on in rehearsal. A production is able to absorb and incorporate such changes. What we are saying is that doing a run of a play is not the same thing as doing three or four performances of it. You have to sustain your performance, avoid tinkering and most important, bring to each show as much energy, enthusiasm and concentration as you did originally.

The stage manager will see to it that you stay on the straight and narrow. Once the director leaves, it is the stage manager's responsibility to maintain the production. This may mean giving the actors notes. Lin Joyce, stage manager: "Actors don't consider the stage manager 'artistic' personnel and find technical notes easier to take than 'artistic' ones. They should trust that the rehearsal period is imprinted on the SM. She was there all the time and knows how you got what you got and why. Many actors have an automatic balk reaction to notes from a stage manager." Kate Greenway: "The stage manager has an idea of the whole picture. Lots of actors are not aware that it is our job to give notes and feel we are 'ordering them around.'" Lauren Snell: "The stage manager is the person who has to keep a perspective on the whole thing. We are the ones who watch every night."

One final point: how ever many times you have done the show, the audience is seeing it for the first time. These people deserve as fresh and vital a show as the first audience to see it. Kate Greenway: "'Just a matinee' is a lousy attitude."

FILM AND TELEVISION

The time frame in media work is tightly compressed. The whole process can take as little as week from the time you audition to the end of your contract.

For an Extra, it can be a matter of a day or so from start to finish. You get the call one day and you turn up at the set the next, wearing one costume and carrying a change of clothes. You sit with your Extra voucher tucked safely away. You are called, you mill about on set, sign your voucher and go home. Being an Extra is an exercise in patience, keeping cheerful and alert while being herded around like a half-witted sheep. It's a real skill and people make a good living at it, but generally it is a means to an end. You may never meet any of the talent (the Principals or Actors) but you will be able to watch some of the work. It is a great way to learn to be comfortable on set. By and large, wardrobe calls ahead of time, make-up and the technicalities of film acting won't affect you as an Extra, so most of this section deals with Principal and Actor casting.

Wardrobe Call

Usually, before your first day of shooting, you will have a costume fitting. Even if your agent has already given them your measurements, someone from Wardrobe will phone you to find out what they are. At the same time they will tell you the time of your wardrobe call. When you get there, you are likely to be presented with a couple of costumes. The first will be impossible to do up, the second will be more likely to fit the star fullback of the Winnipeg Blue Bombers. So much for measurements. Evan Ayotte: "You are not always presented with, 'This is your costume.' You may just have a range of skirts or blouses to try on. They will be acceptable for the broad strokes of the character and Wardrobe will generate something out of it." The smaller the part, the broader the strokes.

Time is short, including the time you are in the costume. Evan Ayotte: "I can make use of pins, *gaffer tape* or whatever for alterations. It doesn't matter. The actor will wear the costume for eight hours, not eight shows a week for four weeks. I haven't time to do proper alterations. I've driven Extras casting people crazy by saying, 'We can't use this actor, he doesn't fit the costume.' It's easier to change the actor than the period evening clothes."

Depending on what you are playing and the size of the role, you are likely to be asked to bring in some suitable clothes of your own. If you are doing a low-budget, non-union film, that request is a certainty.

In union work, you will be paid for two hours at the contractual rate for a wardrobe call, even if Wardrobe has needed you for only fifteen minutes. The money for this call is over and above the fee agreed on for the job. If you are not offered a time sheet at the call, make sure the *AD* (assistant director) adds it to your time sheet on the shooting day.

Script Changes

After the wardrobe call, you wait patiently for the second or third AD to phone you with your call time. During this waiting period, especially on a television series, you may be bombarded with different versions of the script, as re-writes come in. Each set of changed pages will be dated and each will be typed on different-coloured paper. Check the changes. They may be small and techni-cal and barely affect you or they may cut out your favourite scene. Either way, there is nothing you can do about it. Sometimes you don't get these versions until the day you shoot but in any case they make for interesting and colourful reading.

Call Times
It is now the evening before the day you are supposed to be shooting. You haven't heard from anyone. Don't panic. Very often the director can't tell until the end of one day's shooting what the next day's schedule is going to be. Sometimes the shooting schedule is upset because of weather conditions. Just as often, there is a delay because of technical difficulties. (It is a rare television or film schedule that is delayed because of trouble with an actor.) Be prepared for your call time or even the actual day of shooting to be changed. On a union job you will be paid for a changed shooting day unless they tell you a day in advance, but the actual time they want you can be changed, without pay, at a moment's notice.

Finally the call comes, from the second or third AD. *Important: get this person's name.* Write it down. Write down your call, where you are to be if there is transport, when and where the pick-up is to be. Resign yourself to the fact that you may be called as early as 5:30 a.m. and comfort yourself with the knowledge that one day's shooting pays as well as one week's work in the theatre.

Before you go to bed get your stuff ready for the morning. Yes, we know, but your mother was right. You will need:

- Comfortable clothes that won't spoil if they're piled on a chair all day.
- Warm clothes to layer on if needed – you'll feel cold until you are fully awake and television studios are notoriously cold.
- Any clothes or accessories you agreed to wear as the char-acter.

Take off your rings or personal jewellery if you can't wear them in character. Take a shoulder bag or something easy to carry about with you. In it:

- Emergency cash – not a lot because you don't know how good security is going to be.

- Script, character notes, any names of people you have found out, the time and place of your call.
- Light reading, a crossword book, knitting, embroidery, letters – whatever will pass the time quietly and keep you relatively alert while waiting about.
- Lighter and cigarettes if you must; artificial sweetener.
- A toothbrush.
- A little treat in case things start to collapse around you.

You will bless this paragraph when you are trying to kick-start your heart tomorrow in the grey light of dawn.

Shooting Day
You may have a gofer pick you up, in which case, your life is in his hands. If you are travelling under your own steam, arrive even earlier than the god-awful hour you're supposed to. You will need the time to get yourself together. There is total chaos: dozens of people doing incomprehensible things, no one paying you the slightest bit of attention. If you were picked up, the gofer will know where you should go; if not, at least you have the second or third AD's name. You did write it down last night? You did bring it with you? Good. Find someone who doesn't seem to be handling anything vital and ask for your AD. That is your contact, the person you must see before anyone else. The AD will welcome you cheerily and guide you to Wardrobe and Make-up.

Wardrobe and Make-up
This is the one call of the day you can rely on to be on time. Here is a quietly supportive group of experts who see it as part of their job to make you feel good about yourself. This is where you get yourself together and find out how the day is likely to turn out. This is Gossip Control. These people know how the scheduling is going to turn out in reality, who hates whom and where you should be going next. Make friends with these people. They are sympathetic, helpful and caring. Once you have been dressed, made up and combed, you will wait until you are called again.

Waiting
Your wardrobe call (and the make-up and hair calls that will go with it unless you are an Extra) will be about an hour before your set call. Theoretically, you finish there, walk quietly to the set and start work. In reality, you will be ready far too early. With luck, at

this point you may be told to wait in a cubicle in the *honey wagon*, the dressing trailer. More likely, the wardrobe person or AD will point out a communal lounge or three lawn chairs beside a Porta Potty.

On any set, you will do more waiting than working. You will wait to get on the set, you will wait between *shots*, you will wait between scenes and you will wait to be cleared at the end of the day. This is why you brought your book or your knitting. You can't spend all day talking shop to strangers, fascinating though that may be in small doses. Remember, your job is to walk on the set when they want you, ready to give the performance they hired you for. Don't gear yourself up too early for your scene; by the time you get to it, you'll have no energy left. Don't compulsively read and re-read the script; once you have checked with the AD that you have the current version, let your subconscious think about it. Nadia Venesse, dialect coach: "Over-memorizing leads to inflexibility. You'll find it more difficult working with the dialect coach or director if your reading is totally set."

If you want to stretch your legs, make sure an AD knows where you have gone. The worst sin on set is wasting other people's time. Don't make them come looking for you. In some organizations, and depending on the situation, you may be allowed to watch other scenes being shot. This is the best way to learn without the tension of your work being recorded. Nadia Venesse: "Just make sure you stay out of the way. Extras and day players seem to gravitate towards doorways, the worst place you could possibly stand."

Eating

There will generally be coffee and doughnuts around somewhere all day and meals every four or five hours. Try not to go overboard with food and drink. Most actors find it impossible to resist the lure of free food, and the food on film and television shoots is generally excellent. However, if after lunch you have a scene that needs energy, it would be as well to have the blood coursing through your veins rather than sitting in your gut, trying to digest the lasagna you have shoveled down.

On Set

The call comes at last and you head for the set, not forgetting your costume pieces and props and your shoulder bag.

If you are lucky, you will be able to discuss with the director, before you get onto the set, what the scene is about, any questions you may have, any specific route he wants you to take. However, unless your part is of a reasonable size, that simply won't happen. You will be expected to work it out for yourself. According to Gail Singer, a Toronto film director: "Lots of new directors don't know how to direct actors. They don't understand the acting process. In their own training they tend to use fellow directing students as actors. Also, some directors haven't worked on the text sufficiently to articulate to the actor what is needed." In studio work, the director may stay up in the control room and communicate through his floor manager (or first AD).

Down in the studio or out on the location set, you will be appalled by the chaos. Cables in all directions, lights on and lights off, lights humming and occasionally smoking, men and women looking confident and competent, with titles like *gaffer*, *craft services*, *focus puller*, *clapper loader*. Whatever *they* are. *Dire warning: don't touch the equipment*. This is for your own protection. The equipment itself is rarely dangerous but a glare from a union technician can kill at forty paces. Marc Green, sound recordist: "I can't stand it when someone blows into the mike! It puts pressure on the mike it's not built for and it puts moisture in it, which causes static. And it's a great way to destroy my ears."

It is likely they called you as they finished up the previous shot, so that when you arrive they will be setting up the camera and lights for yours. They may have called you early and are still shooting. Obviously, you won't walk into a studio when the "recording" light is on but it pays to be cautious approaching an outdoor set. The staff will be watching for you. Catch an eye and ask where to wait. Wait there. Eventually they will be ready for you. Watch what's happening, get to know how the jobs are done and how many there are to do. Marc Green: "Everyone should know everyone else's job – just a basic understanding, some idea of what and why. That goes for actors, too." The chaos will begin to have a shape. You will see that the director has many threads to keep an eye on. You are only one.

Acting at Last

Rehearsal in film and TV rarely amounts to more than a couple of run-throughs on the set without the cameras *rolling*. Some major directors manage to trade other costly items (a camera crane, more Extras, another location) for a week or so with their leading actors, but this is rare. You can assume that you've got to bring your performance with you. That is true particularly in episodic television. For feature films, you probably have more time. David Cronenberg: "What I like to do is block it just like theatre. We've got our set. So we start reading and working out who goes where. At that point, I'm inviting the actor to participate as fully as he can in shaping the scene. Of course, I'm always keeping the visual elements in mind – what will work and what will not – but at that moment I'm completely open to actors' reactions and suggestions. I'm really happy and willing to consider any possibilities, so I'll take comments and questions. I think it's odd to hire someone you think is good and then not invite them to participate in the movie. You can make mistakes; you can all make mistakes. You can say, after you've shot half the scene, 'You know, it would have been better if we'd left it all sitting on the couch instead of getting up. Let's go back.' You can try different things. It's still the process." We should all be so lucky. But Mr. Cronenberg also understands how things usually work. "Actors must be aware of what the context is. If it's simply, 'Say the lines and don't bump into the furniture,' then do that. If it's one take, then do it. There's no point in trying to turn it into something it cannot be."

Actors are often advised (usually by other actors) not to go full out in rehearsal, to save their energy and emotion for when the cameras are rolling. However, that can cause technical problems. Marc Green: "Actors often won't use their full intensity [of sound] in rehearsals, which is when I have to set my levels. It just wastes time."

You will start with a *master shot*, which sets up a relatively simple framework showing all the action. Then the highlights are added, to be edited in later. Two-shots showing detailed interaction, individual close-ups varying the camera's point of view. This is no time for last-minute bright ideas. The master shot establishes the general trend and the later shots must fit in.

Close-ups are used in two ways: to give prominence to what you are saying and to show your reactions to what is being said to you. In both cases the most important information is being given to the audience by the tiniest changes of expression or tone of voice or where you are looking. You'll need all your concentration, especially since you may be talking to part of the set instead of your partner in the scene, to make your *eye-line* look right for the camera. If you are in a close-up, don't be afraid to ask the cameraman how much of you will be seen. There is not much point in doing something deeply significant if you are doing it out of *frame*. Don't be afraid to admit your ignorance and ask questions. No one is going to think any the worse of you because you don't know what a *key light* is (but see the Glossary). We all have to have a first time.

When you are told to stand in a particular place, or move in a particular way that is where you must stand and how you must move. If it is awkward or feels unnatural, too bad. You are rarely asked to do something without good reason, usually technical, but you are rarely told what it is. If you can find a reason for your character to make this bizarre move, that is great. It will make you feel more comfortable and will probably read better on film. Just don't expect that reason to come from the director.

At the end of shooting a particular set-up, the sound recordist will want to lay down a minute of *ambience*. Every scene has a pattern of sound we don't consciously hear that will be needed for sound editing in *post-production*. If you cough during this minute, it starts again. Marc Green: "It is impossible to get sixty seconds of silence!"

The biggest difference between the media and stage is the possibility of doing a section over until it is as good as possible. At any time during a shot, but generally at the end, you may be asked to do all or part of it over, to do a *retake*. Don't be concerned about the number of retakes that the director decides to do. Most retakes are either because of technical faults or because the director wants to have some editing choices. Remember that every time you do a *take*, it must be physically as close as possible to the previous take. And that includes volume. Marc Green: "Consistency of an actor's readings is so important. Try to keep the volume level the same for each take. It's OK to go from whispers to shouts as long as you do it on the same word each time."

One of the most valuable people on a set is *Continuity*. She (for some reason they are almost all women) is responsible for ensuring that each take looks like the take before. If your sleeves were rolled down and you unthinkingly roll them up before the next take, it is Continuity who gets you to roll them down again. Quite often she will take a Polaroid of you so that there is a record of how you looked at the end of the scene on Tuesday because they are going to shoot the beginning of the sequence the following Monday. This is one reason to stay in position at the end of a shot until you are cleared.

Shooting out of sequence is one of the most difficult things to master. Unlike stage work, where the climax comes naturally out of what has gone before, in film or television the end of a scene can be shot days, if not weeks, before the beginning. An argument in a scene may move from the kitchen to the garden and end in a summer house. The studio set for the summer house is ready now, the location for the garden is available next week but we can't get access to the actual house until the end of the month. Make sure you have a clear idea of the whole script so that you can understand where each shot is in the context of the entire piece. The better you know your character's detailed story, however short it is, in terms of the whole script, the easier it is to pick up shooting at what is for you an arbitrary spot. Gail Singer: "You have to come to terms with the way film and television are shot. You simply can't experience development. You have to find what you can in the scene, the line, the moment. That is what takes incredible concentration. Any development – age, time of day, emotional state – can only be experienced in your script work. You need a very good relationship with your director. The two of you must be absolutely clear and agreed on what the emotional level is every time you shoot a scene." Brigitte Berman: "I've learned about the extraordinary vulnerability of actors. They are relying on the director, when shooting out of sequence, to judge the strength, the emotional depth of a scene."

If you can get it, another aid in shooting out of sequence is to watch the dailies, in film, or the tape of the last sequence, in television.

Dailies

The dailies, or rushes, are all the shots that have been filmed that day, hastily developed and "rushed" back to be viewed to make sure no unforeseen problems have shown up. In a feature film, you certainly won't be invited to watch the dailies unless you have a major role and sometimes not even then. It would take a lot more courage than the authors have to ask to see them. However, on smaller shoots the director is usually quite amenable to having you see the rushes and often invitations are issued to everyone. David Cronenberg: "I always let actors see rushes but I don't think that's very normal. Some actors hate seeing what they do on screen, others are afraid they'll become self-conscious. Some actors thrive on it. The crew can be inhibited if actors are present. It's difficult for me to say to Makeup, 'I hate the way that actor looks' or for the DOP (*director of photography*) to comment, 'Do you see the way the light catches his bald spot?' if the actors are right there."

In television, you can sometimes have a tape played back for you to look at immediately after a take. Even if you are not in a position to ask for that, you can certainly watch other people's scenes on a studio monitor and compare that with the live action. Doing this gives you a general idea of how action and emotion are translated onto screen.

The first few times you see yourself on film or tape, your overriding feeling will be one of deep depression coupled with hideous embarrassment. (Do I really look that awful? Why am I doing so much? Does my nose always twitch every time I start to speak?) or (Why am I the only person who didn't get a close-up? Was I that bad?) Try to be as objective as possible. Learn as much as you can. How far is your idealized version of the scene from the actual image on the screen? How high vocally and emotionally did the climax of a section rise? Where will you have to start that section in order to get to the end naturally and effectively? Nothing teaches as well as actually seeing it in front of you.

Courage, Mes Braves
Don't feel that because your part is so tiny, you mustn't ask for help. Gail Singer: "I want an actor, even a small player, to want to be good. I treat every scene as essential. There could be something vital in a tiny performance that will give you something special on the screen. I don't mind actors asking questions but there are some who would rather talk than do. I welcome questions, suggestions, input but there comes a point when the actor must just commit to doing it. After all, it is rare that there is only one shot at it. Better to make a decision, do it, let the director see it and say yes or no. Give the director a chance to define what it is she wants." Brigitte Berman: "I like to be questioned. Sometimes I get bogged down but a question can open up an area you've not thought about, or enlarge an aspect of the character, physically or emotionally. A small role (whatever that is) is important – a dramatic moment is a dramatic moment. The best films are the ones where the little moments really sparkle. The small-sized characters are quirky and individual, adding a dimension to the scene." David Cronenberg: "It doesn't matter how small the actor's role, I'm happy to listen – if it's honest discussion of the work."

COMMERCIALS
In general, commercials for television are shot in the same way as an ordinary television programme. The biggest difference is the importance of the timing. A commercial is a fifteen or thirty second play to sell a product. Because the time is so short, it is measured to within one eighth of a second. One of the authors once did nineteen

takes of an eight second speech because she was consistently a quarter second too slow! Eugene Beck, a commercials director, says: "You must be a good actor, with the same talent and skills as for any other job plus the insensitivity for commercials! A commercial is a specialty act – life on the head of a pin. A problem is that often an actor is asked to do too much. Commercials tend to be overwritten for the allotted time; advertisers attempt to put too much in. As a result, the actor is forced to speak too quickly and often has to group words together in a difficult or unnatural way."

Because commercials are so short, they deal, even more than regular television, in readily identifiable, recognizable types. Within these types, the clients are looking for "ordinary-looking" people. Gone are the days when only glamorous models were used for commercials, although they are still used for the beauty-care type of advertising.

In all other ways, working on a commercial is like working on an ordinary television programme. The same number of people milling around, the same long waits before you get onto the set. The technician is still king but now the product is the star. Nobody has much of a sense of humour about the writing. Nobody has any sense of humour about the product.

Eugene Beck again: "The best actor is calm, interested, hard working and has a sense of humour. I try to keep the atmosphere on the set easy, there is a lot of tension and anxiety coming from the client and agency. I never yell at actors; it is self-defeating. I keep my direction as clear and as simple as possible. I don't want to scare and I don't want to confuse. I will try to get more specific, starting out with the simplest piece of direction, then adding another piece, then another. I am very aware that time is money and I must do the commercial in a business-like manner. It is art for commerce's sake."

Many actors scorn commercials. Why? Acting in commercials is a skill. The people involved in making them have talent and commitment. Eugene Beck: "It is far better to do three or four commercials a year than to wait on tables. It will give you enough money to get your act together and the freedom to keep auditioning." There are actors who make a handsome living from commercials and enjoy the work. No one is saying it's great art but it is a well-paying, legitimate way to practise your craft.

VOICE-OVERS

Envy the rare, lucky actor with a flexible voice, an excellent sense of time and an agency with a reputation in the voice-over field. For there you have an actor who works all the time, doesn't have to leave town and has a six-figure income.

Voice-over (VO) work is the single most lucrative area for an actor. VOs are used in television and radio commercials, training and industrial films, animation and documentaries. Some of this work is done outside the main centres and you can get it through personal contacts with engagers. Most of it is done in Montreal and Toronto and you need an agency voice-over specialist to get into the field. Even if you have the vocal dexterity and the range of off-the-shelf voices and accents they need, engagers use few agencies.

The VO routine is simple. For a commercial, you arrive at the studio, read over the copy, put on the headset and do it. For a pro-gramme of any length, you get the script ahead of time so that you can familiarize yourself with its shape and content. This may sound easy, and for the VO expert it is, but the skill involved is consider-able.

RADIO

There is little radio drama work in Canada, compared to film and television, and the vast majority of it is done by the CBC. At the moment up to 40 percent of drama programmes originates in "the regions" (a nasty Toronto word for anywhere that isn't Toronto) and 60 percent originates in Toronto. Regional stations also produce drama for the local markets. There are around five hours of network radio drama a week.

Most actors find radio the least pressured of all media work. There is rarely the same sense of urgency and racing with the clock that one feels so strongly on a film set. The process of getting the play onto tape is, from the actor's point of view, a straightforward operation. You arrive at the studio to see that, as on the first day in theatre, everyone except you knows at least one other person. You all sit round a large table with coffee and your scripts. The produc-tion assistant (PA) will pass around a time sheet, which all the actors will unthinkingly sign (see "Be Prepared," page 70), you have a read-through, the director might say a few words, you get up, do a sound check for voice levels, rehearse each scene once on mike and record it. Rarely will you do more than a couple of takes on a scene.

Radio is usually, though not always, recorded in sequence. Sometimes narration will be recorded separately, so that the action of the play isn't interrupted.

Technique

The most important facility a radio actor must have is to "lift the script off the page," which is another way of saying that it should sound as if you are talking, not reading. This is a technique which can be learned (practise with a tape recorder) but a simple trick is to keep your script up at face level, not bend your head to the script. Not only does holding your head up help give the impression that you are really talking, it means that the mike will catch what you are saying. Remove the staples from your script before approaching the mike. Nothing shows up a beginner more than script rustle. The microphone is a sensitive instrument which seems to have a knack of picking up all the wrong sounds, script noise being the worst. Removing the staples also makes it possible for you to carry only the pages you actually need for the scene, leaving the bulk of the script back on the table. Be careful of your breathing. Perfectly ordinary breathing in real life can, if you are placed close to the mike, make you sound as if you are in the final stages of emphysema. If you are close to the mike for an intimate or secretive scene, be careful of "popping." When you say a plosive consonant (*p, b*) too close to the microphone, you overload it and deafen the studio engineer, who is wearing headphones. Your director will let you know if it happens but try to be aware of the danger yourself. It is terribly frustrating to have to do a big speech over again because of an avoidable technical fault.

If you do make a minor error in a speech, most directors like you to pause briefly and go back to a natural break in the speech to do your own retake. Other directors *hate* this. Wait for someone else to show you what the house rules are.

Now that you understand everything about the work process, let's discuss how to make that process as painless as possible.

Chapter Eight
Job Etiquette

"Life is too short to be small."
– Benjamin Disraeli

Love thy neighbour as thyself. That's it, really. If you can remember that all the people you work with, from the lowliest apprentice to the highest-notched director, take pride in their work and have egos that need stroking (just like you), you will have no trouble getting along with everyone.

Actors inhabit a strange position in the business hierarchy. On one hand, we are at the mercy of all – from the producer and director who cast us, to the props, costume, lighting and camera people who can make us look and feel as good or as bad as they want. On the other hand, we are the only really essential people in the business. You can put on a play without sets or costumes or lighting. Try putting one on without actors. Our job is to serve the play through the words and actions of the text. Everyone else's job is to serve the play through serving the actors. Lauren Snell, production director: "The audience is coming to see the play, not the set or the costumes. It's the actors and the words. Ultimately, the whole structure is there as a support so that you can get the best performance possible from that group of people."

The creative and technical staff have the power to free you from worry and allow you to commit yourself totally to the work. They also have the power to make your life a living hell. It's up to you.

Let's see how the "perfect actor" gets through the job.

THEATRE
The Phone Call
You will get a phone call from your stage manager or ASM in pre-production week. Lin Joyce, stage manager: "The perfect actor is always glad to hear from the SM. She asks questions about the first day of rehearsal – where is the rehearsal, is there parking, what's the rehearsal room phone number? She then pays attention when you give the answers. The perfect actor always come clean about anything that might affect rehearsals. She doesn't assume that

the producer has passed on any pertinent information to the stage manager, so she tells the SM that it was agreed she could miss a day's rehearsal because of a film. She mentions allergies, epilepsy, diabetes, any medication. She says that her nursing the baby has been OK'd. Whatever. If the call hasn't come by the middle of the week previous to the first day of rehearsal, the perfect actor calls the theatre."

First Day
Start as you mean to go on. Be on time. On time means early. If a rehearsal is called for 10:00 a.m., it means that at 10:00 a.m. you are working, not walking through the door or hanging up your coat or finishing your cup of coffee. There is never enough time to rehearse a play. Do not waste what little time you have. It can be frustrating to be ready on time and have to wait for the director. It is his prerogative to be late, not yours. He could be dealing with one of a thousand crises. His delay is unavoidable. Your missing the bus is not. Even on the first day, which will probably start out with a leisurely "Meet and Greet," don't be late. Kate Greenway, stage manager: "Time is important. If an actor is late it affects all sorts of other people – the director and other actors, Wardrobe. You're part of a team." However, try as you may, there will come a day when all of nature and technology conspire against you. Lin Joyce: "Call to say why you're late. The SM won't have to worry, will explain the situation quickly and the rehearsal carries on. They won't have to stop when you arrive. That way you waste the least amount of time." When you are late and the rehearsal is going on without you, don't make a lot of extra fuss. Apologize to the SM, unobtrusively if you can, as soon as you arrive. Apologize briefly to the director as soon as there is a natural break.

The first day of rehearsal includes finding out the ground rules. Lin Joyce: "The perfect actor comes to the first rehearsal wearing layers of clothing so that he can either strip off or add on, depending on the temperature of the room, which is never good for everyone! Whatever is decided regarding smoking, live with it. It usually depends on whether the director smokes. If an area has been set aside for smokers, don't crab." On the other hand, even smoking actors accept smoke-free rehearsals. Most smokers are aware that they are now in the unpopular minority and try to be discreet about their smoking. If you are a vehement non-smoker, try to be tolerant.

Costume Problems

In the previous chapter, we discussed the designer's "show and tell." If, after you have seen the costume designs, you are truly concerned about the designer's concept of your role, speak up. (We are assuming here that your part is a substantial one. If you are First Burgher or A Gentlewoman, accept the fact that you are too far down in the hierarchy to voice a complaint about "concept." Fit and comfort should be worked out with Wardrobe. Even fit and comfort may be too much to ask. Safety and cleanliness, however, are essential.) Speak up, we say. But to whom? Phillip Silver, designer: "There is no set protocol of approach to a designer, as long as it is in keeping with the workings of the theatre. The main thing about these discussions is that they should not become confrontational. It is important that the actor listen to what the designer has to say as to why certain decisions were made." Evan Ayotte, designer: "Generally, the first place to begin an approach is after the 'show and tell,' because the designer has just talked through his ideas. If that isn't possible, if you're going straight into a read-through without a break, then in the first fitting. If you feel you have to talk before that, ask the stage manager to set up a meeting between you and the designer or, more informally, just ask for a chat (over a cup of coffee). Send the message through stage management. A good designer will come back to you as quickly as possible."

No one is expecting you to be as articulate about your feelings as the designer may be about the visual concept. Don't let that stop you voicing your concerns, as long as you are aware that you are discussing someone else's creation. Evan Ayotte: "Actors should never feel embarrassed about questioning something they've heard the designer say. A good designer will want to hear what an actor has to say. But it should be direct – not from the actor via the director through stage management."

In the best of all possible worlds, your comments and suggestions would be acted upon. Phillip Silver: "What inhibits a designer's ability to accommodate an actor is often stuff that is not in the designer's control. Some of it may be budget. We've bought the fabric already and we don't have any money to buy more. We've no money to buy the wig that you want or we've bought the wig and I'm going to be in big trouble with the producer if we don't use it. There may be contractual reasons why I am not willing to change your costume. A designer may be paid a flat fee for a certain number of designs. If you have problems and are going to cost me more time to get it right, for which I'm not being paid, I'm not going to be the happiest person on earth. Especially if it cuts into time I should be spending on my next project. In a 'concept' show, an actor may want changes which are absolutely valid but which upset, from the designer's point of view, the balance of the total picture. In most cases, when there are real problems between actor and designer, the only one who can really solve it is the director."

You will be coming into very close contact with design and wardrobe staff, so make sure you have washed and deodorized before a costume fitting. Don't be offended that we mention so "obvious" a thing. Wardrobe people unanimously selected body odour (followed closely by bad breath) as the thing they hated most about having to deal with actors. We forget that the results of our emotional and physical work in rehearsal may be offensive to those who end up with their noses in our arm pits.

Fittings are part of the rehearsal process and should be treated with the same seriousness. Don't be late. Evan Ayotte: "A fitting is not a break. There is a growing number of performers who feel that a fitting is a rest from rehearsal. It's not. The actor must be responsive to the needs of the production. The designer and cutter aren't wearing the costume. You have to tell them if it's uncomfortable."

What do you do if the costume fits, it's right for the character and you just hate it? Evan Ayotte: "A costume is working clothes, a garment that has to perform a function. The designer is always trying to bring the focus back to the character. A good costume will reinforce the basic tools of the actor – his face and hands." Phillip Silver: "When an actor is unhappy, that unhappiness tends to express itself in dissatisfaction with things physical that are close to him. Therefore, it is the costume that doesn't fit or the prop that isn't working, when in fact all the actor is saying is, 'Something is wrong with my performance and how I'm coping with it.' Designers who have been around for a bit tend to understand that. I would say to actors, just try to be aware of what it is that is really bothering you and don't take it out on innocent bystanders." Sooner or later, there will come a time when you have to admit that nothing will or can be done about your costume problem. The perfect actor then dismisses it and gets on with the job at hand. Don't complain about things that are beyond your control – at least not until you get home.

Rehearsals

There are as many ways to approach a play as there are directors and actors. Most drama schools have a strong method of approach, and it comes as a shock to find that other people work in quite different but equally successful ways. Keep yourself open to new ideas and new methods. If the director challenges you in an unfamiliar way, don't cut yourself off. Go with it. Try different approaches. There is no one right way of working.

There are directors who care only about the product. The process is up to you. In that case, work in whatever way you feel most at home. Don't expect other actors to work the way you do but don't feel pressured to abandon your way of working. Many directors don't want to juggle a variety of approaches and so dictate their own. If you find after a good try that you can't work that way, don't attempt to change the director's habits. Don't fight him every inch of the way. Use what you can of his method and then work on your own to achieve what he wants.

Process and product are not necessarily related. We have been in plays where the rehearsal process was smooth, stress-free, exciting and challenging, and the production was dreadful. We've survived rehearsals of trauma by the truckload, feuds and factions, ending up with a thrilling, smooth-running show. Go figure.

The way to keep the process as painless as possible, however weird the approach, is to maintain a sensitivity in your work relationships with members of the cast and support staff. Be aware of technicians' needs. Lauren Snell: "Recognize the human being behind the function." Know when to joke and kibbitz and when to keep your mouth shut. Kate Greenway: "Have a respect for others, for the job that everyone is doing. There is often a schism between actors and crew and there needn't be. The crew want to be part of the team, which they are."

Do your job the best way you know how. Kate Greenway: "Take what you've done during the day. Just thinking about it, assimilating it and bringing something back to rehearsal is part of the creative process." Lauren Snell: "The main thing that makes life easier for stage management is if the actor does his job well, if he is committed to the show. Spend time on the piece outside the rehearsal hall, come to rehearsal with fresh things. Work well with other members of the company. Try not to destroy all the props on the first day! There is something about a person who gives 100 percent of himself that sheds light on the whole process."

The rehearsal period is not an audition. You do not have to compete with the other actors, fight for recognition or impress the director. You have enough on your plate doing what you're supposed to be doing. Concentrate on your character, its development and relationship with the other characters and your relationship with your work mates.

When you have a problem, who do you go to? Start with the stage manager. That's why she's there. Lauren Snell: "If actors go head to head 'artistically,' I have some kind of guideline to follow but if it is just personalities, count me out. Except that these things escalate onto the stage. Then it's my responsibility. The ideal actor retains a professionalism and a commitment to the work that doesn't allow those things to happen." Kate Greenway: "It helps if you can voice what bothers you specifically. If it's technical, it's easy to deal with. If it's artistic, take the stage manager aside. If she thinks you've got a point, the SM will take it to the director. If it's personal, solve it yourself. I'm not a den mother." In most cases, you should be able to approach the director personally with artistic problems, but for a young actor, who may be diffident about doing that, the stage manager is a bridge.

Personal problems between actors need not affect the working relationship. You can play a fight scene with a person you truly like; why not a love scene with someone you really hate? Some of our best work has been with people we wouldn't be seen dead with outside the job.

There is always something in a production that refuses to go right. If the director suggests an "improvement" which you think is no good, what do you do? Try it. It doesn't work? Try it again. And we mean really try it – don't just give lip service to the suggestion. Sometimes a director makes you go over it again and again (as if doing it wrong twenty-three times will somehow make it right). If it still doesn't work and you're First Burgher and A Gentlewoman, our friends at the bottom of the hierarchy, you have to live with it. If you have more clout, you might be able to call a halt and come back to it fresh the next day.

You may eventually have to accept that it simply doesn't work and grit your teeth and do it. Acting, like politics, is the art of the possible. There will be inevitable compromises due to lack of time, money and (other people's) talent. We've said it before. Don't complain about things outside your control. Your job is to make what can work, work. You have only so much time to spare.

Ah, time. That rare and precious commodity. Don't waste it. Be punctual. Learn your lines by the deadline. Do your homework. On the other hand, don't be afraid to ask or discuss. Never feel that you and your part are too unimportant. Let the director judge whether you are time-wasting. Believe us, he won't be shy about informing you. Just be sensitive to the needs of the whole group. Kate Greenway: "A lot of actors want to have a discussion before doing something. This can hold up a rehearsal for ages. Try it first; if it doesn't work, fine, discard it and try something else. Little is solved in the talking."

At the stage in rehearsal when you are ready to go off book, be careful how you ask for a prompt. Some actors snap their fingers at the stage manager or ASM when they need a line. Don't. You can say "Line" or "Yes" or "Please" or "Damn it, what's the line?" or all sorts of things but don't snap your fingers. It sounds rude and peremptory, and most management personnel dislike it. And we don't blame them.

Prop Perils

If during the rehearsal process you and the director agree that your character needs a particular prop, ask for it as soon as possible. Lauren Snell: "Stage management usually catches that sort of thing in rehearsal but let them know just to be safe." Lin Joyce: "You have to phrase a request so that the person understands that they are your equal, your partner, not your personal valet. Always [make your wants known] in the form of a request, not a demand." But be sure your character does need it. Kate Greenway: "If you're having trouble with a scene, don't add a prop. It puts pressure on the department to get something for the actor and it is usually cut. If it is a legitimate request – the scene would move better, it sets up an interesting interaction between characters – then it's no problem."

As rehearsals progress, the workshops and Wardrobe will begin to produce the more important costume pieces and props to replace the mock-ups stage management collected for rehearsal. When you are presented with a prop, don't look at it suspiciously and ask, "Is this it? How am I supposed to work with this?" Lin Joyce: "Accept a costume or prop graciously; the costume or prop person who made it is usually there. Even if it's awful, try to restrain your glancing wit so that you don't destroy the person." Bob Baker, the Canadian Stage artistic director: "How would you like it if after the first read-through a prop person approached you with his face in a grimace, saying, 'Is that the way you're going to do it?' No one expects the actor to get it right first time. Don't expect any more from the support staff." Lin Joyce: "Remember, it's not finished. Hold off those cheap shots! Be willing to work with it for the balance of that day or the following day. Before saying anything, try to think through the problems so that they can be articulated clearly. Notes that are taken from that are the notes that will make it right. 'Too small' – does that mean it's uncomfortable, it hurts, it restricts movement? Be specific. [Also] be super honest. If you are uncomfortable with something emotionally, say so. 'It makes me feel peculiar' won't make people think of you as a raving neurotic. You don't have to use things that make you feel terrible. There is usually a way of modifying it to make it OK." (But remember what Phillip Silver said about costumes. Make sure it is the physical object and not your work that you're worried about.)

Notes
Note-taking is an integral part of the rehearsal procedure. Traditionally, notes are given by the director to the actor – not by the actor to another actor. Notes are the director's criticisms and suggestions, based on a run-through. There are three things you never say in response to a note:

- "But I did that!"
- "But you told me not to do that, yesterday."
- "I would have done that but Miriam was late on her cue."

Never explain, protest or whine. And never, *never* blame someone else, even if you are justified. You may say that you don't understand, once, and expect a rephrased version, but that's about it. Notes are not for debate. They are given at the end of the day when people are tired and tempers are frayed.

If you really have a problem with a note, ask the stage manager or the director about it afterwards. If you get the same note repeatedly, it is probably because you think the director is saying one thing and he is actually saying something else. Ask for an analogy or an example or a different explanation or a line reading or anything. Otherwise, you both are wasting valuable time.

Tech Week
Lauren Snell: "Tech week is hell for everyone. It is hell for the actor moving out of the warmth of the rehearsal hall onto a stage that looks nothing like those coloured pieces of tape on the floor." Lin Joyce: "By the time tech week arrives, the perfect actor is exercising the patience of Job." Lauren Snell: "Remember, rehearsals have gone on for two or three weeks; you are very familiar with the piece. The operators and crew have only had verbal briefings by the ASM or have just been told to hit a button at a certain time. They don't really know what the piece is. They don't get to know until well after opening." Lin Joyce: "Techies are working like things demented.

The gratitude of techies towards an actor with class is enormous and you develop a great company bond." Of course they won't always get it right first time. God knows, you didn't. Lin Joyce: "Even if they do get it right first time, it's only luck and they'll screw it up the second time!" Lauren Snell: "There will be a day or two when changes happen constantly. The best rule is to continue to do what you have always done unless told to do otherwise. Don't change your timing to adapt to somebody else. They are changing, trying to adapt to you! You'll never meet."

Lauren Snell: "Keep a sense of humour. It is a trying week that doesn't have to be made worse by people having their biggest tantrum ever. That is the week people do it." Lin Joyce: "If you do give in to tiredness and decide to have a tantrum, forget it, you've broken the bond. The crew won't accept tantrums from each other and they won't accept them from a performer. If you do fall from grace, you must apologize publicly. Then you have a fighting chance of getting back into the crew's good books."

Lin Joyce: "If you can only extend yourself to go beyond being patient and be grateful! It is so unusual for an actor to turn to a *dresser* and say, 'I'm really glad you're here.' Or to pass a lighting man in the hall and say, 'I know you've got about 250 cues; I think you're fantastic.' They need to hear it. The only recognition technicians get is from directors, stage management and actors." Kate Greenway: "There is an attitude among actors that the people behind the scenes really want to be actors. It is important to realize that there is a pride and a skill in what they do. There is also a love of what they do and actors should recognize it."

First tech day is dangerous. There is still a lot of work to be done on the set and only the stage manager is in touch with all the departments. Today, she is in charge, more than the director. Kate Greenway: "Don't walk all over the set, open doors and complain that there are no railings. When you arrive, sit in the house for the SM's ten-minute chat. She will warn you about incomplete and possibly dangerous spots. Cords exposed will be taped, dark areas will have light. The crew are experts. Trust the stage manager to look out for your safety and health." Unfortunately, not all stage managers are as punctilious as Ms. Greenway. Make it your own responsibility to check the safety of everything you will be asked to do, in rehearsal as well as in performance. This needn't be confrontational but you're the one who will fall down the hole where the stairs were supposed to be. Yes, that happened to one of us.

Make sure that all potentially dangerous moves, scene changes, special effects, etc. are gone through slowly and carefully before you do them in costume at performance speed. Moves in darkness must be rehearsed in light, explosions and gunshots must be demonstrated while you watch from the house, someone else must be hanged with the trick noose. Insist on more than one layer of safety; an actor was rushed to hospital from a Stratford production of *Julius Caesar*, stabbed in the lung despite protective padding and a retracting knife. It's your body, it's the only one you'll get. You can protect yourself without a major row. Don't say you won't do something, angrily; say you can't do it, regretfully.

A warning about costumes: during the tech dress, you will be sitting around in your costumes for ages. Do be careful of wrinkling, dirtying, spilling coffee and dropping cigarette ash. Someone who is already overworked will have to clean up and iron anything you have dirtied and wrinkled.

Be prepared to wait for no apparent reason. Lauren Snell: "In a Q to Q, it seems as if there are long periods where nothing is happening. But something is. People are adjusting sound and lighting levels, discussing cues, the necessity for *cue lights*, timing." Don't disappear – keep yourself available.

Props and costumes should arrive in time to be tried in performance conditions and improved if necessary before your first audience. Fall on everything with cries of joy. Wardrobe is working eighteen-hour days and needs all the praise it can get. Make notes as you use things on stage and find out the problems. List your wants in order of importance. Decide (1) what you can't do without, (2) what you really want and (3) what would be kinda nice to have. Delete (3). Now look at (2). Now delete it. We're left with (1). Assuming there are no more than three things in (1), you can only be disappointed three times. That's reality. If you haven't received your requested item by opening night, you won't be getting it.

Being a classy actor has helped you get through the strains of rehearsal but the benefits continue. Lin Joyce: "The support system network is strong and widespread. Directors ask stage managers all the time about actors – what are they like to work with, do they make trouble?"

Opening Night

If you are planning to give tokens of thanks and/or good luck, this is the night for it. (An exception: some actors prefer to give "Last Night" cards or tokens. That way you have unpressured time to think about the perfect trinket.) Never feel obliged to buy First Night cards or flowers or wine or anything else. If you want to, great. If not, no one will think the worse of you. However, if you give cards to your fellow cast members, you must also give them to the support staff. They had as much to do with getting the production on as you. In a theatre with a huge support staff, you don't have to give something to each person. A good rule of thumb is to give something to a department as a whole (e.g. Wardrobe, Props) and something else to any individual who specifically worked on your costume or prop. Remember to take extra cards to the theatre on opening night. You are bound to have forgotten someone.

Not everyone considers First Night to be Fun Night. Many actors prefer to treat it the way they treat any other performance, and you must respect that.

After the show, which we are assuming you have survived – most actors do – there is usually a First Night party. Although you are no longer on duty, as it were, be polite to the members of the public who have paid good money to see you. It is only common courtesy to listen civilly to whatever drivel is being aimed at you and, who knows, your patience may be rewarded. You might find yourself in a rousing discussion about the play and end up with an invitation to drinks or lunch or an afternoon aboard the family yacht. It's happened to us!

And speaking of drinks, try not to overindulge. You've got another show to do tomorrow.

The Run

And another. And another. The stresses of opening night now give way to the pressures of keeping the show running smoothly. You are required to be at the theatre at "the half" or half an hour before the show starts. (Some theatres use the British "half" which is actually thirty-five minutes.) Many actors arrive long before that to give themselves time to let whatever has happened during the day wash away in the ritual of preparation.

In a room that is over-crowded and over-heated (or under-heated), dressing room diplomacy is a number one priority. The authors, easy-going in the extreme at home, are Dobermans when their counter space is threatened. Woe betide the actor who invades our territory. Two inches of Kleenex box in our make-up area and it's straight for the jugular.

Actors prepare in different ways. If you like to do a full physical and vocal limber before you make up, find somewhere other than the dressing room to do it or do it at home. The actor sitting quietly in the corner with a crossword and the daily paper may be preparing for the performance as well.

Some actors are superstitious. Some superstitions – the ones you believe in – make sense. Others – the ones you don't – don't. Whether it is quoting from *Macbeth* or whistling in the dressing room or having real flowers on-stage or whatever, be diplomatic and patient with the actors who are affected by the superstition.

Wash your pits, brush your teeth. Remember, small hot spaces make for all sorts of nasty body odours and that makes for rows in the weeks ahead.

Outside the dressing room, as part of your preparation, check all your props. Lauren Snell: "Lots of older actors check their own props. I used to find that quite irritating. I used to think, 'Why do they do that when they know we're doing it?' Now I realize that it's their way of going through it. They may have had an experience where something wasn't there." It's all in how you do it. Check at a time when the pre-set has been done. Never move a prop from where it has been set. Let Stage Management know when things get worn or fragile. During the run, stick to the same routine with a prop so that the ASM knows she can collect it from the stage left prop table where you left it, instead of finding it behind the bin where you threw it.

You are getting bored with doing the show the same way night after night. Too bad. You have a contractual obligation to perform the play as rehearsed. There is growth from continuing to think about the play and an inevitable change as audiences differ. Lauren Snell: "As sound and lighting people become more familiar with the nuances of the show, their performances change as well." But, in essence, the production remains the same. Lin Joyce: "If something never worked and everyone knows it never worked, there is room within the performance to get it to work. An actor should go to the stage manager before trying something new. You never know if cues depend on it." In the same way, actors should expect to be told when Stage Management makes or authorizes changes. You have the right to expect everything on the set and on your costumes to remain absolutely unchanged, or be given the chance to see and work with the change ahead of time.

Whatever else you may want to change, *never change fights*! Kate Greenway: "Fight scenes – weapons, any difficult or dangerous move – a hit, a jump, a blow – all these should be run through before the show without fail. Always make eye contact. Do it step by step, technically, not 'acting.'" When there is stage combat of any sort, the best theatres will have a qualified fight director to choreograph the routine and work with you in rehearsals, a fight captain to maintain the fight through the run, a fight call before every show and someone whose job it is to check and repair the weapons and lock them away every night. If you are missing even one of these (which you probably will), it is an added danger.

It is the stage manager's job to keep the show going as it was directed. She is entitled to give notes to that end. Lin Joyce: "The perfect actor requests notes, 'Any notes for me?' It's best if it becomes an exchange. The stage manager can go into the dressing room after the show to ask for notes (torn costume, wobbly prop) and give notes in return." Lauren Snell: "Actors often resent notes. It's really hard giving them. Actors should know that. I'd rather have a show with a million cues than actors whom I know are going to be hell on notes." Be gracious when receiving notes from the stage manager. All the advice for responding to notes from the director applies to those from the stage manager.

It is hard to be gracious when a technical error has made you look like a prime idiot in front of five hundred people. However tempting it is to blow a gasket at the nearest bystander, don't. Lauren Snell: "It is such a sensitive profession and so difficult to mend a breach. Count to ten. You usually blow up at the first person you see – the apprentice, then the ASM – and you're reasonably calm by the time you see the stage manager. If you've got a problem, don't walk up one side of the apprentice and down the other. It's not fair. At least the SM can defend herself if it's an unreasonable blow-up. And if it's reasonable, it's the SM who should be getting it, anyway. It's nice if the operator who made the mistake goes down to apologize as well. But ultimately, it's the stage manager who must take the heat."

Try to accept the apology in good grace. It's not easy for anyone to admit he made a mistake. Don't make it any more difficult by being a Neanderthal.

In turn, if you do something wrong, whether to your fellow-actor or to a support staffer, apologize immediately. It's gracious and grown-up and it's the most effective way of defusing a potentially explosive situation. Lauren Snell: "It's gratifying to get an apology from an actor but it's the information that's useful. 'I think I hit something in the blackout.' It's good to know that an actor doesn't panic in a crisis."

Try to anticipate problems. Lauren Snell: "It's helpful if an actor can show common sense in an emergency. If you know about a crucial prop placement, you should think about what you'd do if it wasn't there one night." Kate Greenway: "If something goes wrong on-stage, even if it's not your responsibility, try to deal with it." People appreciate the quick-witted actor whose antennae are always working.

All the problems of being the perfect actor are increased tenfold when you are on tour. Normally, you can get away from your co-workers, explore new places on your own once rehearsals are over, and have a life outside the theatre. On tour, you are trapped with a small number of people for weeks – sometimes months – on end, and it takes all your tact, sensitivity and class to keep a positive working relationship with them all.

Your Reward
What is the reward for being the perfect actor? Lin Joyce: "People cannot wait to work with you again! There is a star system inside the stage management and technical world. Our stars are the people we love and admire and who love and admire us."

FILM AND TELEVISION
Actors starting out in film and television rarely have more than a day or two on any job. Not much time to knock the socks off anyone. But plenty of time to screw up.

Wardrobe Call
Be prepared to be there the full two hours of your call. Lots of actors, knowing that wardrobe calls are generally less than fifteen minutes long, book themselves doctor's appointments or lunch dates or auditions and then are upset and anxious when the call drags on. Don't take the chance. Also, don't fume because you were called for two o'clock, arrived in plenty of time and now have to sit around because everyone else was called for two o'clock as well. Think of it as a dentist appointment without the anxiety and with pay. That is the point, by the way. They are paying you for two hours of your time. So don't grumble, read a book. Or talk to the other actors. It's an excellent opportunity to meet and break the ice with your work-mates before your shooting day.

Wardrobe call will be your introduction to some of the most helpful people on the set. It's part of their job to make you feel good about yourself. This does not mean that your costume will necessarily fit. As long as it looks all right for the camera and isn't too uncomfortable, accept the fact that sleeves will be shortened with safety pins. Find something to praise – complaints are not well-received. Wardrobe departments are notoriously overworked and under-staffed and often deal with fifteen or twenty people at a time. Keep cheerful and relaxed. If a skimpy jacket is the worst thing you have to endure, offer prayers of thanks, not whines of discontent.

Call Times
No one likes getting up at oh-my-god o'clock in the morning. When the second or third AD phones with your call time, don't wail at the unreasonableness of the hour. At most, you may allow a slight piteous whimper to pass your lips. Otherwise, it's a straightforward and cheerful, "Thanks, I'll see you then."

Shooting Day
Get there in plenty of time. You may have to search around for the exact location. The parking lot may be a quarter of a mile from the actual set. It may take you some time to find anyone who knows who you are, what you should be doing and where you should be doing it. Your first job is to find the AD who phoned with your call time and whose name you should have written down. Any AD will do in a pinch (they all have those walky-talky things and will get in touch with the one you want) but it's best to report to the person who made the first contact. That AD will get you to Wardrobe, Make-up and Hair.

Wardrobe, Make-up and Hair
Even at o-my-god o'clock, you have no excuse for turning up without having brushed your hair and washed. Shave if you're a man, don't put on any street make-up if you're a woman. If you have to be extra nice to anyone, these are the people who deserve it. They are artists in their own right and yet are open to (well-chosen) comments or suggestions. They accept that you are more familiar with your own face and hair than they and will ask about hair partings and make-up colours. Don't tell them what to do but if they ask for input, don't be afraid to give it. Nicely.

You are likely to be in costume for hours before you ever get onto the set. Don't wander about. You must be available and your whereabouts known at all times. Someone will show you where to wait. And there you stay, unless you tell someone. Hurry up and wait is the order of the day. And it is bad manners to complain about it. Nadia Venesse, dialect coach: "I have never heard a principal player complain about having to wait – only the day players. You're being paid good money to read or do a crossword. Why complain about it?"

Rehearsals

There's one thing you can rely on in media work: you're on your own. You have been cast because you can deliver the goods. It's up to you to deliver them. If you are lucky enough to work with a director who is willing to talk and listen to the actors (like the directors in this book) you are ahead of the game. Most directors will give you technical direction and that's all. Accept the situation and give the director what you gave at the audition – that's why you got the job.

Be particularly sensitive to the needs of the technicians. The technician is King (only occasionally Queen); be respectful, don't offer an opinion, pay compliments and if necessary shine shoes. This doesn't mean you can't joke and kibbitz. Just know exactly where your place is in the hierarchy. W-a-a-a-y d-o-o-o-w-n.

Shooting

You will be asked to do impossibly awkward things. If they are shooting someone's reaction to your words, you may be crouched out of frame, with your face squashed into the side of the camera, so that the person in frame will be looking in the right spot. Try to give full value to your off-camera lines – it's what you would like in return. If it is your shot and the other actor is sitting in the star's trailer, you may be doing all this great acting to the floor manager's hand, while someone drones the words at you. There is no point getting upset about either of these situations, or any other. You do what you are asked promptly, efficiently and without any game-playing.

If, for any reason, you are not having a good time, keep it to yourself. A set is a dangerous place to shoot off your mouth, no matter how quietly. Marc Green, sound recordist: "A mike is a very sensitive piece of equipment. I can eavesdrop so easily on actors. Whispers come through clear as anything!" Be warned.

Your Wrap

When you have finished (*wrapped*), make a point of going around to all the people who have had anything to do with you and thanking them for their help. It doesn't have to be a big production number. Just a quick and simple, "I'm wrapped now, so 'bye and thanks for everything." People appreciate being appreciated.

COMMERCIALS, VOICE-OVERS AND RADIO

There is one admonition that is common to these three areas of work: *Don't knock the copy.* However inane or infantile you consider the script, keep quiet about it. Without exception in commercials, most of the time in VOs and frequently in radio, the person who wrote this garbage is sitting right beside you. Or at least within hearing distance. These scripts are not first drafts. They are the result of discussions, meetings, re-writes, client input and several bottles of Valium. And that is usually how they read. However, you have been hired to say the words, not comment on them.

A special word about commercials: *Don't knock the product.* If you are morally outraged by it, you shouldn't have auditioned for the commercial. No one is asking you to believe in the product. But they are paying you to be polite about it. Why antagonize a potential source of revenue?

There. The perfect media actor. Any sane agent should jump at the chance of representing you. Let's go.

Chapter Nine
The Ten Percent Solution

"To manage men, one ought to have a sharp mind
in a velvet sheath."
– George Eliot

WHAT IS AN AGENT?

The actor/agent relationship is like a marriage. You can only find out if it's good for you by trying it. All we can do is discuss the problems and pitfalls, what you should expect, and your part of the deal. Abe Isaac Greenbaum, former assistant national director of the ACTRA Performers' Guild writes: "An agent is a person who works for and on behalf of another person."

JOB DESCRIPTION

Knowing what an agent is doesn't necessarily bring us any closer to understanding what an agent does. The agent has several job responsibilities:

*   Reads plays and casting breakdowns (film and television casting needs) from casting directors, CBC.
*   Puts the client's (actor's) name forward to casting directors, theatre directors and producers for parts.
*   Negotiates the terms of the client's contract.
*   Counsels and advises a client on career decisions.
*   Consults with a client on relevant financial matters.
*   Deals with problems between actor and management during work.
*   Acts as an intermediary between client and management.

According to one actor, "Your agent is hired to say the things you are too scared to say yourself." Shari Caldwell, Toronto agent: "An agent is a necessary luxury, an intermediary, a buffer. Someone who stands between the actor and the engager without getting in the way." Sandie Newton, Edward G. Agency: "An agent is a sounding board, a buffer, a control."

For these services the clients pay the agent a percentage (normally 10 percent for stage and 15 percent for media work) of their gross professional income. This percentage is commonly called a commission although, more accurately, it is a fee. Money paid to an actor for expenses (accommodation, travel, transport of pets) is not income and therefore the actor does not pay commission on it. Actors should pay commission on a job to the agent who originally handled it, no matter how long ago the work was done. Twenty years ago one of us had a four-week job from which the agent is still taking fifteen percent on residuals.

What an agent does not do is get you work. Celia Hamilton, assistant branch representative, ACTRA Toronto Performers: "It is a false view, held by even mature actors, that agents will get work for you." An agent gets you work opportunities – auditions and interviews. It is up to you to get the job.

Unless you live within striking distance of Vancouver, Toronto or Montreal, you may not get an agent to take you on. If this is the case, read the end of this chapter, pages 137–38, "Is an Agent Necessary?" People may suggest you also need a business manager and a publicist. Eve Brandstein, in *The Actor*: "Get a dog instead, it's better company."

EXTRAS AGENTS

Background performers are often hired through extras agents, especially in the three big centres. They are actually closer to the casting agencies (see page 138) in that they simply organise your bookings and don't counsel or protect you. You still pay them fifteen percent, however. In this chapter we are talking about *talent agents*.

AGENT VS. PERSONAL MANAGER

In the United States, there is a significant legal difference between an agent and a *personal manager*. In Canada, the terms are practically synonymous. Bruce Ward, 21st Century Artists, says: "In Vancouver, 'agents' are responsible only for looking for work and negotiating contracts, although they may do more." A 'personal manager' has all the responsibilities listed on page 123. In this chapter, we will use the word "agent," since it's shorter.

EXCLUSIVE AGENCY

In Canada, your agent represents you in all your acting work. You may do other work (modelling, writing) for which another agent may represent you. With the exception of Extra agencies, it is rare that a personal manager or agent will agree to take a percentage from only part of your acting income. At the time of writing, the

Talent Group in Toronto is the only agency we know of that is actively working to end exclusive representation.

BASIC PHILOSOPHY AND ATTITUDES

The most important thing to remember is that your agent works for you, not vice versa. You are paying for the agent's time and expertise and should expect value for money. Respect the special knowledge the agent has but remember you are buying that knowledge. Too many actors are intimidated by their agents. Don't be. Ann Summers, director of the Canadian Resource Centre for Career Performing Artists, says in her book, *Getting It All Together*: "A manager is not Mr. Fixit or Wonder Woman but a professional tool to be utilized and appreciated rather than feared and resented."

Career decisions are up to you, not your agent. Don't give your agent that power. In fact, most agents won't accept the responsibility. Penny Noble, Noble Talent: "I will give advice if it is appropriate to do so but the decision is the client's." Sandie Newton: "Advise a client on a career move? We will discuss it together. I can give both a professional and a personal opinion, but I never make decisions without consulting a client. David Karnick, David Karnick Management: "I don't insist that the advice be taken. [If it isn't taken] too many times then maybe I am not the right person for them." If you find you are consistently not taking your agent's advice, think about changing agents.

The agent is a sounding board. Discuss the pros and cons of a career choice with your agent, who usually can predict and understand the consequences of that choice. You will find that simply talking it over with the agent will clarify the situation in your own mind. Sometimes, you will find that you needed someone to say "yes," for you to realize that the right answer for you was "no." There is no need to assume that your agent knows better than you what's good for you. What you should expect is a more cool-headed, less emotional approach than you might have.

Good agents look after many careers, diligently and well. You look after only one. Believe us, no matter how much interest an agent professes in your career, *no one* is as interested in it as you should be. (Except your mother.) And no one has as much to lose. This is a fact of life. Daryl Jung, music columnist in *NOW* magazine: "No matter how sincere or involved a manager appears to be, rarely do they stand to lose as much as bands."

You and your agent should form a team. From Ann Summers, *Getting It All Together*: "An investment has to be made on both sides.

Neither artist nor manager can sit back and wait for things to happen." Bruce Ward: "Don't expect an agent to establish a career. You'll only be disappointed." It is your career and you are responsible for it. Gary Goddard, Shari Caldwell, Sandie Newton and others say: Keep in touch, network. The agent is part of your support staff. Actors have got to sell themselves; they can't just sit there. They are part of a promotional package. The agent can't do all the work. Stuart Aikins, casting director, says there are actors who, "now that they have an agent, sit back and wait for the phone to ring. I don't believe that's the way love, life or the arts work."

The agent's reputation is on the line when you go up for a job. Shari Caldwell: "The actor is representing the agency to the casting director, producer, etc." Sandie Newton: "Clients also represent the agency. If they screw up, it is a reflection on the agency and the other clients it represents."

THE AGENT-CLIENT RELATIONSHIP

The agent-client relationship is a business arrangement. It must begin with discussing, defining and agreeing on the areas of work and responsibility. The agent is acting on your behalf, so you need to know that this person is honest, forthright and has your interests at heart. By the same token, you must not lie to your agent. Any gains made by lying to impress an agent are short-lived. Be frank about your ambitions. Gary Goddard: "Much of the relationship is intuition and chemistry. Discuss what you want your agent to do. Where you want to go. You and your agent should be on the same wave length when it comes to the aim and thrust of your career. You've got to be headed in the same direction, aiming for the same goals." Shari Caldwell: "Talk to your agent generally about the business to give him a flavour of your concerns and interests." An open, honest relationship is the most effective.

Stuart Aikins: "I do think the actor should establish up front with his agent the philosophy of how they work. That should include informing casting directors when people are working and what they're doing. Most good agencies do that."

Be sure you know what the agent will bill you for. The majority of agents we spoke to said that the actor pays for material supplies (photographs, résumés, voice tapes, demo tapes) and the agency pays for long distance phone calls, postage and courier services (unless – and they all added this – it is to send a photograph and résumé to a casting director because the actor forgot to take them to the audition!) Sandie Newton: "It is the client's job to supply the agency with the ammunition to sell her. On long distance calls, I am usually representing more than one client, so the agency pays for it. But if I am specifically requested by the client to make the call, the charge goes back to the individual."

Within the limitations of a business arrangement, there are great variations in an agent-client association. Gary Goddard: "In my case, client relationships run from purely business to business and a close friendship. It makes no difference in terms of the work I do." Shari Caldwell: "Friendship is fine but it only goes one way. The actor feels able to call on an agent for personal help but the agent can't call on the actor."

Whether your relationship is close or formal, you should be able to voice dissatisfaction and concern. Although you must trust that an agent is working for you, you shouldn't be afraid to ask for an accounting of time and effort. And a good agent shouldn't resent the request. Cultivate your agent; get to know how your agent works. Can you call for a chat? Does calling every day break into the agent's routine? What hours does the agent work? A good agent shouldn't mind clients keeping in close touch. Call your agent after a job or an audition to keep the agent up to date and informed. Gary Goddard: "Chasing your agent or not depends on your personalities. Some of my clients communicate daily, others much less frequently."

Agents should make their expectations clear from the outset. Sandie Newton: "I expect my clients to be professional, dedicated. They should be spending the same amount of time and energy on their careers as I am." Penny Noble: "I expect co-operation, enthusiasm. The recognition that every chance is precious. They should be accommodating, prepared to be inconvenienced. I expect them to be well-prepared and do the best possible audition." Lawrie Rotenberg, The Talent Group: "I expect professionalism – the way they handle themselves, the tools they provide, their own approach and energy to the business. I want frankness, a career relationship. Sensitivity helps. Teamwork." David Karnick: "I expect dependability. Show up for an audition; tell me if you are going on vacation. If there is a conflict, say so. Wear the right wardrobe; get the copy in advance; be punctual. Provide me with up-to-date and sufficient photos and résumés." Bruce Ward: "Read all the script if it is available, not just your part."

CONTRACTS AND POWER OF ATTORNEY

Ann Summers, author of *Getting It All Together*: "A contract between manager and artist ... is a written statement of a verbal agreement."

Talk it all over first. Whether or not there is a written contract, you must be perfectly clear who does what.

Is it necessary to have a written contract with your agent? Yes, according to Abe Greenbaum, in an article in *ACTRAscope*, Fall 1988: "Authority for an agent to act is either by written contract or oral agreement … Unless you contractually limit the scope of the agency, you may find that … your agent does something of which you do not approve and you will have no legal recourse. With a contract, you will be able to specify [in] what kinds of matters the agent may act on your behalf (with or without your prior consent), [in] what types of contractual relationships the agent may enter on your behalf and what, if anything, your agent may do with fees paid to you and sent to the agent.

"If you have no contract with your agent it will be very difficult to protect yourself if your agent does something wrong or something you feel was beyond the scope of your relationship. If there is no contract and you sue your agent, the court will look to industry practices of what agents do, and judge your case in that light."

Mr. Greenbaum makes a good argument for the need of a written agreement, and yet there are scores of actors, the authors included, who have been in the business for over twenty years and have never had a contract with their agents. The size and the power of the agency have nothing to do with contracts. Oscars and Abrams, one of the most powerful agencies in Canada, whose clients' gross incomes exceed four million dollars, has no written contract with its actors. Richard Brooke, agent: "No contract – ever. We must have full trust. A verbal agreement is binding. A contract is superfluous. If an actor wants to leave, he'll leave." Penny Noble: "At the moment I don't have a contract with my clients but this may be changing. I have never required it, but as Toronto grows it may become necessary. I have a good relationship with my clients; we respect one another. I am entertaining the idea."

It seems that even agents who use contracts consider them more of a way to avoid misunderstanding than as a binding agreement. Lawrie Rotenberg: "We use the standard [ACTRA] contract. It's not much, really. Simply the sign of a relationship. I have never held anyone to it and will let people go. In the future, the *profession* may move to an enhanced contract." Says Christopher Marston, executive director, Canadian Actors' Equity Association: "A contract with an agent is always dissoluble immediately. Only a vindictive agent would want a dissatisfied client on his list. Termination terms should be reasonable – take legal action if you're worried." (In

Toronto and Ottawa, call ALAS – phone numbers, page 199).

The authors feel happier not having contracts with their agents but it is a personal choice. If you have discussed every aspect of the arrangement and you feel comfortable about signing a contract that puts in writing what you have agreed to verbally – and nothing more – by all means, sign. If you are unsure of signing and the agent insists, maybe that is the wrong agent for you. Never let yourself be pressured into making a decision quickly.

Power of Attorney, as used by agents, gives them the power to sign the client's contracts or cash cheques made out to the clients. Abe Greenbaum: "The power of attorney is a contract which provides that one party signs certain rights or powers over to another person [allowing that person] to act as if he or she is the person who gave the power. [The document] will have provision on how the relationship may be ended and what can and cannot be done under the power of attorney." This authorization can be as limited or as general as you allow. Be sure you understand exactly what the agent's Power of Attorney covers. If you're not sure, take the form away and read it again. If it is still confusing, have a lawyer explain what it means.

Not all agents want Power of Attorney. Lawrie Rotenberg: "Most of my clients have given me Power of Attorney. But it is not necessary if they don't wish to." Penny Noble: "The cheques come into the office made out to the client so I need Power of Attorney to deposit the money. I may have to sign a client's name to a contract. Most clients prefer it. It saves them a trip to the office." David Karnick: "I don't have Power of Attorney at the moment. It's not necessary. I use the opportunity of swapping cheques to see clients, discuss things. Power of Attorney is good if an actor is shooting abroad for weeks and cheques come to the office. But it is an enormous trust. The manager must respect that trust." Richard Brooke: "I don't have Power of Attorney. I don't want to handle all the actor's income. I'm not a business manager."

As people who want to have a firm handle on their own careers, the authors would prefer to give an agent no Power of Attorney. We like to be paid for the work we do and *then* pay the commission we owe. We feel that actors have a responsibility to read their own contracts and understand them before signing them. After all, if an error or omission slips through, you are the one it is going to affect, not your agent. We know it's great to have someone else to blame but is it worth it? It's up to you.

HOW TO APPROACH AN AGENT

Getting an agent is like getting a job. You do your research, you send your photograph and résumé with a covering letter, you phone to set up an appointment, you follow up and you keep trying. David Karnick: "The covering letter is more important than the résumé. *Never* use 'Dear Sir or Madam.' This is an insult. You're saying you are doing a mass mailing, not applying directly to me. You should be doing research on the agent. *Don't spell my name wrong.*" Lawrie Rotenberg: "I'm not too worried about the form of the résumé coming in. Content is more important just for clues – the weight of roles they've carried, the people impressed enough to hire them. Try to get someone you have already impressed to contact the agent." Don't be shy about asking friends to recommend you to their agents. If you can mention a well-known name in your letter, and especially a current client, an agent will probably give you more consideration. Ask your teachers, if they are active in the business, and directors you have worked for. Penny Noble: "The more professional the résumé the more it grabs your eye. I look at the content of the résumé before I look at the photograph. It has to be in the ball park with the rest of my clients, who have very strong experience. I already have a demanding list. If the actor is just beginning, I probably won't have time to see him. An exception to that is a young actor with great training. Always write first. We send a form letter back, returning photograph and résumé. We will phone if we're interested but it's fine if the actor phones us."

Always say in your letter that you will follow up with a phone call. If your phone call results in no appointment, don't give up. Remember, agents receive up to a hundred photographs and résumés each week. Out of those, very few actors will be seen. Try again in a few months' time. The agent's situation may have changed by then – actors leave agents, new agents join an agency, agents' needs change. If an agent leaves the door open for you – "Why don't you call again next spring?" – take advantage of it. If you are coming in from out of town, write before you leave and phone after you arrive, if you see what we mean. As with all business calls you make, work out beforehand what you plan to say. And concentrate! You are often put on hold for so long that by the time the agent gets on the line, you have forgotten who you're calling and why.

If you are in a show – workshop, showcase, school, professional – invite the agent to come to it. Be sure to give plenty of notice. If it is not free, offer to provide tickets. Lawrie Rotenberg: "I go to school performances as often as possible." Agents are busy and can't see many shows but offering tickets gives you a reason to call and follow up the letter. If you have a demo tape, you will want to drop it off with your résumé and letter. If you are lucky enough to get an interview with an agent on the strength of your first package (photograph, résumé, covering letter), be prepared to audition or do a cold reading.

As for any interview, come well-groomed and presentable, in your own personal style. You should look your best even if you have just arrived to drop off your résumé. We know of at least one case where the agent was walking through just as the actor was handing her résumé and photo to the receptionist. The interview took place then and there! Don't expect that to happen but go dressed for it.

Be on time (or phone as soon as you realize you are going to be late). Politeness and consideration are rare commodities in this business and make such a pleasant change.

Be courteous to the receptionist. Many will pass on their comments before the agent even sees you. Actually, you don't know that it is the receptionist; it could be one of the agents. You will probably have to wait, so use the time to get a feel of the agency. Chat to the receptionist if there is a break in the phone calls, look at the eight-by-tens of the agency's clients, check the bulletin board for the reviews of their work. Don't make a nuisance of yourself, just keep your antennae working.

Be prepared to be criticized. This is not personal and not for debate. Re-style your hair, lose or gain twenty pounds, shave the beard, get new photos, fix your résumé – it may sound abusive but all it means is that the agent is not willing to represent you in your present state. Don't be offended. Don't feel that you have failed. Accept the comments and give them careful consideration. You may decide that the agent is all wrong, in which case, try another one. You may decide that the agent is right, in which case, re-style your hair, lose or gain twenty pounds, shave the ... etc. and try again when you can show the agent the new you. In either case, follow the interview with a thank-you letter and stay in touch.

Above all, remember that the whole scene is fluid. New agencies are forming; agents are breaking away from the original group to set up on their own; actors leave agencies, creating holes that need filling; the industry's casting needs change as fashions in character types shift from year to year and season to season. Don't be discouraged. Circumstances change and persistence pays.

HOW TO CHOOSE AN AGENT

Before you can choose an agent, you have to know what your choices are. A possible choice is not to have one. Not having an agent doesn't mean you aren't professional; an agent is sometimes necessary, sometimes useful and sometimes a complete waste of time. (See pages 137-38, "Is an Agent Necessary?")

If you are going to be based in Toronto, read *An Actor's Guide to Agencies in Toronto*. This slim volume comes out twice a year and lists all the agencies in Toronto with names and addresses, a brief description and a general evaluation. The book is published by Moonlighters Publishing and is available at Theatrebooks. (See page 200.) A word of warning: the information about an agency "not presently expanding its *roster*" may be out of date. There is an inevitable time lag between getting the information and publishing it, and situations change.

In the States, the performers' unions franchise agencies, signing them to a demanding list of responsibilities. As a member, you may not use an unfranchised agent. In Canada, anyone can set up an agency and our only protection is actors' word of mouth. Actors in Toronto will soon be protected by the Code of Ethics of a new agents' association (see page 135). We assume you won't be tempted by Tillie Henrietta O'Malley's Charm School and Intergalactic Talent Agency. There are plenty of different sorts of legitimate agents to confuse you.

A large agency, with more than about three agents, tends to have a more extensive network of information and more contacts than a small agency. On the other hand, a small agency may be more inclined to hustle for you because you aren't lost in the crowd. A top-ranking high-powered agency may be able to get you in to see more important people – but a new agent may be more motivated to try.

Within the large agencies, there are individual agents with separate rosters of clients whom they represent. Each generalist or *programming agent* has thirty-five or more clients and looks after film, television and theatre. The agency may also have one or more "specialists" who put up all its clients for commercials or voiceovers. An advantage to this set-up is that the actor has the use of someone who has special knowledge in a particular field. But it also means that, for that field, each actor is one out of over two hundred clients and there is less chance of a personal commitment.

Ultimately, what really counts is the single person who will represent you. Bruce Ward: "Do your homework first. Know what you want an agent to do." Do you want a professional who works with you, for you, or one who tells you what to do? You are not only finding out about the agency, you are also telling the agency what you want and need.

Look for the total number of clients that the agent represents. If it is more than forty-five or fifty, you are not going to get much of the agent's attention or commitment. It will be spread too thin. Most good agents have between thirty-five to forty-five clients on their lists.

Who else does the agent represent? Find out from *Face to Face* or ask the agency. If you know any of the clients, phone them up and ask their advice. Tread carefully in this area and remember what works for one person may not work for you.

If an agent asks for money up front, run, don't walk. Agents make money from their percentage of what you make *after you make it*. Any agent who asks for money before that is not legitimate.

Beware of agents who insist that you use the agency photographer. Although an agent may suggest one or more photographers, the choice should be up to you.

Some marginal agents also run "schools," which they suggest will make you more successful. Some make more money from the schools than from commissions.

Beware of any agent who advertises and any who guarantees work.

Listen to your gut. Go by intuition. Go for the person who you feel is most concerned with *your* career, *your* problems, *your* success. Agents who feel wrong are like a pair of ill-fitting shoes – they get less comfortable, not more, with time.

How an Agent Chooses You

Penny Noble: "Seeing the work is best. If I am familiar with their work in film, TV or theatre I won't need a demo tape. I very rarely interview before seeing their work. An exception to that is seeing a very full résumé with interesting work, or a recommendation of a casting agent. Even so, I will still want to see a tape before I make the final decision. Sometimes I go to the theatre to see someone. In that case, we will just need to talk. I have to be impressed enough to sell them. If I'm not 100 percent convinced, then I can't get behind that. Before demo tapes were so widely used, I used to ask for audition pieces."

Sandie Newton: "I will choose on the basis of referrals and interviews. If the actor has no demo tape, I will ask for a monologue."

Lawrie Rotenberg: "I try to see their work. Film, television, live performance. A demo tape, if nothing else."

David Karnick: "I'm interested in a look, a good instinct. Work seen is not a criterion. The experience is on the résumé. If you cut yourself off, based on someone's experience, you are cutting your-self off from helping to develop talent in the industry."

Shari Caldwell: "I won't audition actors. I like prospective clients with effective publicity to get in. It means their work-publicity philosophy is good."

Richard Brooke: "What is their work like? I will consider someone because of a recommendation by another actor, by being approached and interviewing them."

Bruce Ward: "The only real criteria are, one, can I communicate with them and, two, can they act? Conflicts on my roster don't enter into it. That's the casting director's area."

WHAT AN AGENT LOOKS FOR

Lawrie Rotenberg: "In general, it is a combination of gut feeling of talent and energy, and references. Salability. Marketability. Do they fit into the market as it is? I have to consider my own needs. Are there conflicts on my roster?"

Penny Noble: "I look for the charisma, excitement. When you see it in an interview – the warmth and enthusiasm – it draws you."

David Karnick: "They must be of an appropriate age group for the roster. Never more than three people in any five-year age range. There should be an element of "commercialism" in order to sell. Pleasant, appealing, non-offensive. I don't want a roster of all one type but there is the question of supply and demand – what is out there and what is wanted. I couldn't take on every talented person who came to me. I will recommend other agents to people."

Shari Caldwell: "I have all food groups on my roster and I am careful to avoid conflict. Do I like the person?"

Richard Brooke: "Can I sell them? Do I have any conflict on my roster? Do I like them? Can we have a working relationship?"

Gary Goddard: "Taking a beginning client relies on pure instinct."

IS YOUR AGENT WORKING FOR YOU?

It's almost impossible to tell, because the amount of work, even the number of auditions, depends so much on whether the market happens to want you. Here are some areas where a bad agent may fall down:

- Can you reach your agent on the phone? Are your calls returned promptly?
- Do you feel encouraged and optimistic after talking to your agent? Or have you had to listen to your agent's problems?
- Do you seem to know more about what's going on than your agent does?

- Is your file kept up? Correct home and work address, and phone numbers? Plenty of good-looking résumés? Are you warned when photos are beginning to run out?
- Can you ask who the agent is contacting on your behalf? What you are being put up for?
- Does your agent come to see your work in theatre and know when you are appearing on television?

The Standards, Ethics and Practices of a 1989 organization, the Talent Agents of Vancouver, includes:

CODE OF ETHICS (some examples)
The Talent Agent shall

- Conduct himself or herself with honesty, courtesy and good faith toward all parties;
- Represent Clients with integrity, honesty and confidentiality;
- Solicit prospective Clients only in an honourable, reputable and professional manner;
- Endeavour to obtain payment on behalf of the Client as expeditiously as possible.

OBLIGATIONS OF AGENTS (some examples)
The Talent Agent agrees to

- Counsel or advise the Client in the advancement and promotion of his or her professional career;
- Be truthful and disclose all pertinent facts;
- Make every effort to negotiate above minimum fee for the Client;
- Inform the Client of the known terms and conditions ... and to obtain the Client's consent, before confirming or make binding any ... commitment on behalf of the Client;
- Advise the Client of all known information pertaining to each ... engagement;
- Seek out and confer with producers, engagers ... for the purpose of securing work for the Client;
- Maintain proper records;
- It will be the responsibility of Agents to define their services to their Clients and ensure that any Client is informed of their role in a business relationship.

The document deals with fees to be charged, how clients will receive their cheques, services such as distributing promotional material, exactly how Power of Attorney is to be used, and much more. The organization is now on hold but the document was the starting point for a similar code being developed by Toronto agents, in discussion with ACTRA Toronto Performers Branch.

We asked some Toronto agents what their clients should be able to expect from them. The words we heard most often were: availability, energy, frankness, interest, professionalism, sensitivity, leadership, guidance, time, effort, dedication. (We should be so lucky.)

WHEN TO LEAVE YOUR AGENT

All actors go through bleak periods. It can be comforting in such times to blame your agent for lack of work or work opportunities. It is not necessarily the agent's fault. You might not change your luck just by changing your agent. Gary Goddard: "Be cautious when deciding to change agents. Talk it out with your present agent. It could be something solvable."

At the other end of the spectrum, actors often want to move on to an agency with more prestige after they have gained a modicum of recognition and success. Again, exercise caution. Shari Caldwell: "Changing agents after success is common but it doesn't often help. A new agent always takes six months to work effectively for you. Being put up for casting doesn't differ much between agents." Brian Levy, casting director: "It is possible to outgrow an agency. Don't let being 'friends' affect you. But don't change agencies just for 'prestige.' If your agent is getting you auditions, money and billing, why move?"

How do you know when you have outgrown an agent? Is it wiser to stay with an agent who knows you, understands you and has worked hard for you? Is your agent powerful enough to represent you now that you have become well-known and sought after? Shari Caldwell: "Top agents represent stars, writers and directors, and will hear of projects and have some say even before a casting director is contacted." It is reasonable to assume that a casting director will start by looking at casting suggestions from agents with the best reputations. Brian Levy: "The prestige of the agency doesn't matter a bit. What does matter is the individual I'm dealing with. There are some agencies I won't deal with but not because they are newer or smaller. It's because they give me hassles ... and basically aren't pleasant to deal with."

How much does personal loyalty enter into it? David Karnick: "I would encourage any performer who can do better elsewhere to go. Don't allow personal loyalty to overshadow business. I can do more if the actor is committed."

If an agent is not representing you the way you want to be seen, if you're not being put up for parts where you feel you have a chance, if your agent is repeatedly discourteous, unavailable and unwilling to listen attentively – it's time to leave. Talk it over and try to work it out first but if it is impossible, make the break.

However angry you are at your agent, leave the agency amicably. Shari Caldwell: "Leave the door open in case you need to return."

Although it is certainly safer – and much less frightening – to have found a new agent before leaving the old one, it is often better to have no agent than one who is harmful to your career.

Anon, in the *Penguin Book of Modern Quotations*: "Changing agents is like changing deck chairs on the Titanic."

IS AN AGENT NECESSARY?

According to agents, the answer is a resounding "yes," as an access to media casting. According to actors, the answer is a resounding "sort of," as a buffer and negotiator.

In Vancouver, Montreal and Toronto, work on union productions is closed to you if you don't have an agent. Casting breakdowns are sent to agents, and casting directors consider only the suggestions the agents make when they draw up audition lists. Not all agents will be able to open many doors for you in theatre. Their strength is in getting information quickly and knowing everyone important. They can do this in the media but you can do it as well as they can in theatre. Once the offer is in, your agent should negotiate effectively in any field. The times are changing, though, and there are different points of view. Certainly we find now that more and more theatres are sending breakdowns to agents instead of relying entirely on annual general auditions and callback. Chris Marston, Canadian Equity executive director: "An agent is helpful for media work but a beginner is not helped in theatre work. Agents may treat small theatres [where beginners tend to work] high-handedly and lose their client an ill-paid but interesting job. Agents are helpful with richer, distant management and in tough negotiations, where they can compare your ability with others'."

When you are a younger, more inexperienced actor, agents know your market value better than you do and have a better idea what the market will bear. Richard Curtis, in *How to Be Your Own Literary Agent*: "A lawyer who represents himself has a fool for a client. As my own client, I tend to be impatient, to have no objectivity about my own work and to be so flattered that someone wants to publish me, as to accept terms I would sternly reject if they were offered for one of my author's properties."

Although they may have a better overall view of the business and a more reasoned perspective, agents certainly aren't necessary. In fact, if you live and work outside the three big cities, Toronto, Montreal and Vancouver, the question doesn't arise. There are no agents. A theatre or radio job (and even some television) comes to you directly; other media work comes through a *casting agency*. The casting agency – the Other Agency in Edmonton is a good example – is hired by the production company to bring in actors for casting sessions. The Other Agency will contact the actor directly. The agency is paid by the production company and the actor does not pay the agency any commission. If there is any negotiating of fees or conditions (and there often isn't), the actor deals directly with the production company.

Although there is not an enormous amount of feature film work cast outside the three major cities (except in Alberta), there is plenty of local television, radio and film work, especially industrial, educational and in-house film and television, plus a large theatre market, to keep you pleasantly occupied. The occupation is made all the more pleasant knowing that 100 percent of the fee goes directly into your pocket!

Chapter Ten
All for One – but is it for you?

"Yes, we must, indeed, all hang together or, most assuredly
we shall all hang separately."
– Benjamin Franklin

This chapter is about the performers' unions. They are in fact professional associations but they carry out most of the functions of trade unions. They negotiate with groups of engagers, developing Agreements which lay out minimum standards of working conditions, hours and pay. The unions police the Agreements and resolve problems between performers and engagers. They provide health and accident insurance and a retirement plan. They are there to protect their members' interests and to promote and maintain high professional standards. Theoretically.

It is possible to have a career as an actor without joining the unions, especially outside the major cities. As a non-member, you can still work in union theatres and on union sets, and enjoy union work conditions. The most important thing is that, once you have joined either performers union, you may not do *any* non-union work. You are cut off from working in student or professional non-union films, non-union TV commercials, community theatre or professional non-union theatre without the unions' specific permission. Before you decide to join, talk to union officers, or at least write to them. ACTRA has offices across the country (except in New Brunswick, Prince Edward Island, the Yukon and the Northwest Territories), and Equity is based in Vancouver and Toronto (see Addresses, page 194). Union people are marvellously approachable and can give you all the information you need. This is just a quick overview.

In Canada, there are three performers' unions: ACTRA, Equity and UdA. The first two are anglophone unions and the third is francophone. We are mainly concerned with Equity and ACTRA.

ACTRA
ACTRA is made up of three Guilds: Performers, Writers and Media. The Performers Guild, through ten autonomous local branches, represents actors in film, television and radio, and has over twenty different Agreements with engagers.

All the Agreements cover these basic matters (and much more):

- Minimum payment – a higher fee may be negotiable.
- Licence to use material in specific markets or for defined periods.
- Minimum fees for re-use of material (residuals).
- Basic work conditions, hours, meal breaks, etc.
- Overtime, subsidiary payments, penalty payments.
- Bond to secure artists' payments.
- Engager contributions to ACTRA health insurance and RRSP through ACTRA Fraternal (see next page).

If you are a member of ACTRA, you can get a copy of any Agreement from your local ACTRA office. If you get it and read it you'll know what you are agreeing to when you sign a contract. And what the Engager has to do. Which seems like a good idea.

The Performers' Rights Society polices residuals and royalties here and abroad. ACTRA member or not, PRS will go to bat for you, although there are many occasions – when a production has been sold, for instance – where they can't do much. If you are an ACTRA member and you hear that your face is on screen again in an old production, contact the ACTRA office before the PRS. However, do make sure ahead of time that (1) you weren't working as an Extra, (2) you haven't already been paid, (3) you didn't sign a *buy-out* and (4) it really was you on the screen. Whatever you do, do not take anyone else's word for it that one of your old programmes is back on the air, unless they can tell you the name of the programme and where, when and on what station they saw you.

When you are working in ACTRA jurisdiction, you must receive your money within fifteen working days of doing the job (it's about three weeks) or else the engager incurs a *late payment* penalty. Non-union engagers pay when they're good and ready – another advantage of a union.

ACTRA on Set

ACTRA stewards are employees responsible for a specific type of work. By visiting as many sets as they can, they head off problems before they affect the members. More like the Equity deputy (see below) are the OSLOs (On Set Liaison Officers). These are ordinary union member volunteers, selected and trained by ACTRA. OSLOs receive expenses and a daily fee, for which they monitor the set and call the steward when necessary. Any member can call the steward directly (the union guarantees anonymity) if an Agreement is being breached.

Do think before you call on the union; there may be a simpler way to set things right. Don't phone the ACTRA national executive director about the lack of toilet paper in the washrooms, as once happened, when a reasonable request to the department concerned could solve the problem. However, we know of actors working in near-freezing temperatures who have been loath to complain, not wanting to "jeopardize their jobs." This is the sort of thing the union wants to protect its members against.

Joining

Before becoming a member of ACTRA, you may work in a union production by paying for a *work permit*. The payment depends on the size of your part and where the production is going to be seen or heard. After your first permit, you will be sent an Apprentice Member Kit, giving you a chance to participate in ACTRA, but not to vote, and to build up the six permits (three if you are in a visible/audible minority) which qualify you for full membership. Extra permits don't count and apprentice membership costs $30 up front and $30 annually. Apprentices may not work on non-union productions, so think carefully before cutting off that source of work.

If you are already a member of Equity, you can join ACTRA immediately; in fact, you may not work on non-union media contracts. As a member of Equity you may automatically become a member of ACTRA with your first professional media engagment. As a member of Equity, you only have to pay half the ACTRA initiation. If your first engagement in ACTRA's jurisdiction is in an Extra category, or where the full fee is less than a hundred dollars, an Equity member may pay initiation fees and dues by instalments.

Costs

At the time of writing, the ACTRA initiation fee is $300. If you are already a member of Equity, you get in for half this, plus your first half year's minimum dues. You pay initiation once, at the beginning; dues go on forever.

ACTRA Fraternal Benefit Society

ACTRA Fraternal takes care of the members' health and dental care plans and their retirement funds. The health and dental care plans supplement your provincial health plan – the more you earn, the more they cover. Of course, you really need more help the less you earn. But whoever said life was kind? You can buy extra coverage but it's hard to make money from an insurance company.

Your ACTRA RRSP starts when you join the union. Each union engager deducts 3 or 4 percent of your fee, adds its own equal contribution and sends the total to ACTRA Fraternal. These contributions are locked in until you reach retirement age. By having funds locked in, and through good management, the ACTRA RRSP has an enviable record. You can start a voluntary RRSP plan, make extra contributions and withdraw those funds with no trouble.

CANADIAN ACTORS' EQUITY ASSOCIATION

The CAEA, better known as Equity, started life in 1955 as a branch of Actors' Equity Association of the United States (AEA). It did not come into its own until April 1, 1976, when it separated from the AEA and became a completely independent and autonomous body.

Equity has around forty-seven hundred active members, who include actors, stage management, directors, ballet and opera performers. Equity represents all these involved in live, unrecorded performances.

With some exceptions, Canadian Equity contracts refer to the CTA (Canadian Theatre Agreement), which is an agreement between Equity and the Professional Association of Canadian Theatres. It determines hours of work, minimum pay and working conditions, and sets down rules, regulations and responsibilities for both artist and management.

Before a theatre may receive contract forms for a show from Equity, it has to post a bond with the union. This bond guarantees that Equity members will receive two weeks' salary plus benefits in lieu of notice should the employer suddenly run out of money, for whatever reason. A comforting thing, don't you think?

The Equity Deputy

All Equity productions have a deputy, elected by the Equity members of the company on the first day of rehearsal. The union says the deputy is "your representative and the direct link between the Equity members of the company and the Equity office." The union stresses that a deputy should never become involved in confrontation with management. The deputy is not an employee of the union, as the ACTRA steward is; he or she works with the stage manager to avoid potential CTA infringements and reports them to the Equity office. The deputy represents the cast's interests, and is not responsible for dues-paying, timekeeping or discipline. At the end of the contract, the deputy ensures that all members have been paid in full, including travel money and any overtime owed, reports same to Equity and signs the Deputy Release form in order to release the bond to Management.

Non-Professionals
Equity theatres are allowed a certain percentage of non-union actors in a production but non-Equity theatres may employ union members only in strictly limited circumstances.

Joining
The easiest way to become a member of Equity is to be offered an Equity contract. The theatre may offer an Equity contract to whomever they wish. You may be offered a contract simply because the non-union quota has been filled.

If you are already a member of ACTRA and have been offered work in an Equity production, you must join Equity. If your stage experience is limited, Equity may allow you to register as an apprentice.

Apprenticeship
You may apply for Equity membership under the apprenticeship programme. The programme requires that the apprentice work with an Equity company in a minimum of three productions in twenty-four months, not all with the same theatre. You work as a non-professional, without Equity's protection, insurance or minimum salary. You file, along with your registration, a fee of $100 for each production. At the end of the two years, if you have completed three productions, you pay the balance of the initiation fee (at the time of writing, the initiation is $675) and ask to join. This must be done within six months of the end of the two years. At any time during your apprenticeship, if someone offers you an Equity contract, you can accept it and join straight away.

The American Equity apprentice scheme guarantees classes and workshops, but in Canada all you have is the opportunity to work in a union theatre and learn what you can. With rare exceptions, you will simply be a gofer for anyone who needs help, on- or off-stage.

You may decide that the profession really is as dreadful as your teachers, parents and this book have tried to tell you. If you give up the stress of the theatre (and join a bomb-disposal squad, for instance) or if you do not complete three apprentice jobs in two years, your $100 fees are forfeited.

The one bright spot in those two years is that as an apprentice, you may attend Equity auditions, thus losing out to a better class of actor.

Costs

As we said, the initiation fee for Equity is $675. If you are a member of ACTRA, you are allowed to deduct your ACTRA initiation fee to a maximum of half the Equity initiation. Don't forget that after you've figured out the initiation fee you still have yearly dues to pay.

The RRSP and the Accident/Sickness Insurance Plan

You must apply for your RRSP when you join. The theatre deducts 3 percent of your gross wage from source and contributes an equivalent 3 percent. Your insurance coverage includes your travel to and from the contracted job. While you are under contract, you are covered twenty-four hours a day, on or off the job site, basically for the medical, surgical and job-loss results of accidents. The engager pays the insurance premium.

UNION DES ARTISTES

The Union des Artistes, or UdA, is the union which covers stage and media francophone work. The union represents around four thousand actors, most of whom are based in Montreal. You join UdA by work permits – thirty of them – and by indicating that you can function in French. The reciprocal arrangements with Equity and ACTRA are rather complex. Roughly speaking, ACTRA and Equity members may work in UdA jurisdiction (and vice versa) three times a year under courtesy work permits. If you want to know more about UdA, get in touch with their local offices (addresses on pages 195 and 202).

WITHDRAWAL

Now that you know all about the unions, how do you get out of them? If you have been going through a rough time and don't feel like paying dues when you haven't worked for months, you can go on Withdrawal or Inactive Status. You don't pay dues, you no longer have a vote, you can't attend meetings but you are still considered a union member. Which means you cannot, while on withdrawal, do any kind of theatre work. Or television. Or film. Or radio. Or anything. Union or non-union. Professional or amateur. Nothing. Nada. Nitchivo. The moment you act for the public, however far removed from union theatre or media it may be, you must reinstate yourself in the union, pay any outstanding dues, be under the relevant contract and be paid for your services. We cannot make this point clear enough. Once you are a member of a performers' union you can *never* act for *any* company without the knowledge and permission of your union.

RESIGNATION

Leaving ACTRA is easy enough. You simply resign and it is as if you had never joined. You may re-join at any time if you pay initiation dues like a new member. It is Equity's policy to discourage resignation. If you resign, you will have to give up your professional career formally in writing.

THE ALL-IMPORTANT QUESTION

Should you join the performers' unions? And if you should, when should you? (All right, that's two questions. So, sue us.) The answer to the first question is reasonably straightforward. Yes. If you are serious in your desire to become a working professional actor, you will eventually have to become a member. The business has grown and matured since its amateur beginnings to become a complex structure with international connections. It is theoretically possible to make a career as a performer without ever joining ACTRA or Equity but in order to pit yourself against the best in the industry, to protect yourself against devious and exploitative engagers and to get the most lucrative work, you have to join the unions. In the union you can have your complaints against management handled anonymously and you have knowledgeable people on your side. The union can only be as strong as its members but it is bound to be stronger than an individual actor.

When to join is something else again. All we can say is, not until you have to. Actors feel that by joining a performers' union, they have in some way "made it." Not true. It is better to have interesting credits on your résumé than simply union membership. By joining Equity and ACTRA early on, you cut yourself off from challenging amateur, semi-pro and non-union professional experience early on in your career. Christopher Marston, executive director, Canadian Actors' Equity Association: "Non-Equity companies may be useful to a new actor. They are likely to offer an actor bigger roles and more responsibility than an Equity company would. You have more chance to compare companies and ways of working. Don't be in too much of a hurry to join the union. Once you're in, it's hard to get out, except permanently. Media casting rarely depends on having ACTRA membership. If you're right for the role, they'll cast you."

Please, don't rush this decision. Unions don't get you work. They protect against much of the exploitation of actors but they don't get you work. Find out about the non-union opportunities in your area. The Equity theatres probably have non-union general auditions for small parts. Outside Ontario there are masses of non-union commercials being done. Get in touch with provincial arts councils for lists of community and non-union professional theatres. Theatre Ontario (address on page 200) has lists of professional theatres, union and non-union, across the country. At last count, there were 122 union theatres and 217 non-union theatres. And those are only the established professional companies. An actor without a track record will be welcomed and given important work by a new company that values commitment and enthusiasm. Contacts you make when everybody in the group is struggling can stay with you throughout your career. Amateur and community theatres, volunteer entertainments and student film-makers offer opportunities as well. Remember, once you have committed yourself to the unions, there is no turning back.

KICKBACKS

"Kickbacks" are, in the authors' opinion, among the nastiest and most exploitative realities of this business. From the CAEA membership information pamphlet: "Kickbacks occur when anyone gives back part of their contractual salary to a producer or where anyone agrees to receive less than their full contractual salary."

Never, repeat *never*, allow yourself to be treated in this way. From a 1983 Equity newsletter: "Don't be pressured by threats that another actor is at the door if you don't agree. Report the matter to Equity – it will be dealt with confidentially and you will stop the employer believing he can exploit performing artists unchallenged. Once you have signed to perform and the engager has signed to use you, you both have obligations to fulfil. Don't let a dishonest producer make a profit by taking your salary." Agreeing to hand back some or all of your money is agreeing to theft. Not only does it cheat you, it cheats actors to follow.

As long as you are not a union member, you are free to work for nothing, or for that matter, to pay the theatre to let you work. It's up to you. But when you join a performers' union, you take on an obligation to defend the rights which people before you fought long and hard to obtain. If you find that difficult to understand, you are not ready to join a union. End of lecture.

We have added the following unions so that you won't feel like an idiot when the initials start to fly.

IATSE

The International Alliance of Theatrical Stage Employees and Moving Picture Operators of the United States and Canada: IATSE (pronounced eye-at-see and also called IA) is a union of nine hundred locals covering technicians, front-of-house staff, camera operators, costume designers, dressers, etc. Only larger Equity theatres are unionized, though all ACTRA work is.

NABET

The National Association of Broadcast Employees and Technicians is a rival union to IATSE and started as a reaction to IA's nepotism. (Going to an IA meeting is like going to a family reunion.) Unlike IATSE, NABET is strictly a union for workers in the media.

ACFC

The Association of Canadian Film Craftspeople was started in 1979 in Toronto and is just now forming locals in Vancouver and Winnipeg.

UBCP

The Union of BC Performers split from ACTRA in 1991. Recently, after much negotiation, the BC ACTRA Performers Branch and UBCP decided to get back together as an ACTRA Performers Branch.

UNION STRENGTH

Our Agreements spell out fair working conditions and the union tries to see the Agreements are upheld. They are not always successful. Weak unions? No, weak membership. When you allow a rule to be broken and don't complain, the union can't police the rule and it will die. If you disagree with a particular policy, get involved; run for office. It's the members who make the rules, the staff who enforce them.

If you want a strong union, you can have one. The strength of the union is the only protection you have against engagers abusing their power.

Chapter Eleven
Fitness

"Perfection is such a nuisance that I often regret
having cured myself of using tobacco."
– Émile Zola

A good carpenter wouldn't dream of working with dull or rusty tools. A successful realtor won't show a dirty house. An actor worthy of the name, working or not, must have a supple, finely-honed instrument responding to its owner's needs. That instrument is the most complex mechanism known to man: the human body and mind.

PERSONAL FITNESS
Health
All the exercise classes in the world can't do anything for a body that is being abused internally. Get enough sleep, don't smoke, don't drink to excess and, for God's sake, stay away from drugs. We know this sounds like your mother but she's right again. One of the few advantages of acting as a career is that there is no mandatory retirement. As long as there is breath in your body, strength in your limbs and a neuron or two in your brain you can continue. But once your wind has gone, your limbs wracked with injury and your brain with coke, you're finished.

Start as you mean to go on. Be sensible about your body. We've all heard about college football stars who limp along through their adult lives after toughing out knee injuries. An actor can't afford that. If you have a sore throat, do something about it right away. Unless you plan to become a mime, you can't get away without good vocal equipment. If you have over-indulged in drink, smokes, or M and M's, back off for a while. No one is expecting you to wrap up in cotton wool or live the life of a monk but just be aware that the body is only so resilient. And gets less so.

You should also be aware that a reputation for being unreliable through heavy drinking or drug taking is easy to establish and difficult to shake. David Cronenberg, film director: "You want stability. It's very common for directors and producers to check with others on whether an actor is an alcoholic or a druggie or is neurotic. Life is too short to use a wonderful actor who will hurt other aspects of your film. You weigh all those things."

Speaking of weight, don't ignore diet in your never-ending search for the healthy life. Touring, living in digs without cooking facilities, working on films with fabulous catering (including wine and beer), working weird hours – all these are great excuses (and sometimes reasons) for wolfing down everything that's smaller than your head. Find ways to get healthy, balanced meals on a regular basis.

Working among strangers, living alone far from home, means you have to be responsible for your own health. We can't advise you to become an actor if you have physical problems like diabetes, epilepsy or major allergies, although there are actors with these conditions and more (one of your authors is a diabetic). Come to that, we wouldn't advise you to become an actor even if you were as fit as a fiddle.

You should know your body and its problems. Carry enough necessary medication, wherever you are. Inform someone in authority about your condition if it might affect the work. Lin Joyce: "The perfect actor comes clean about anything that would scare stage management half to death if they don't know about it ahead of time."

Try to get back to the same health professionals for preventive maintenance. See your dentist regularly: actors need their teeth in the worst way.

Please don't become a full-time hypochondriac. That's the worst sort of dressing room bore.

Fitness

Assuming your insides are squeaky clean and functioning as they should, how do you best maintain your outsides? Almost any kind of exercise is good for you as long as you do it consistently and don't become an exercise bore. Actually, being an exercise bore isn't so bad for you as it is for your poor friends, who have to listen to how many reps you did or laps you swam or how high your pulse rate was in aerobics class. (We know about this. One of the authors was an Exercise Bore until the other author threatened to cite the Y in a divorce suit.)

Exercise that uses the whole body in an aerobic activity – swimming, rowing – is probably the best but only if you do it all the time. It is better to walk briskly every day than to do a more demanding exercise at irregular intervals.

Exercise makes your body flexible and toned. It gets oxygen-rich blood moving, lowers blood pressure and it's great for the complexion. It also eases tension. The high you get from a good work-out is real and physiological. Even if it weren't, who cares? Physical activity makes you feel good. Things don't look so black when you have just set a personal best in your bench presses or finally managed to do a whole length of the pool without needing CPR.

Working out also helps give a structure to your day when you are not acting. As Tallulah Bankhead once said, "Exercise is good for the heart, the lungs and the unemployed."

WORKSHOPS AND CLASSES

Exercising the body is good; exercising the body and the mind together is better. Most actors continue to study after entering the profession. Throughout the country, there are opportunities to keep your skills sharpened. Voice classes, audition workshops, improv classes, scene study, script interpretation, Shakespeare classes, acting for the camera, singing – all these and more are available to professionals and non-professionals. At a basic level, if you lack a skill completely, community colleges have Continuing Ed classes in the evenings, city parks and recreation departments often hire professionals to teach, and some theatres run classes. Private classes and private schools vary in their standards. Before you sign up for a series, you should be able to audit a class. Check out classes with friends who have attended in the past.

Some classes are open to professional actors only. Many schools bring in teachers with national and international reputations. Vancouver has Workshops in the Performing Arts, Saskatoon has the Saskatoon Arts Guild, Halifax has Workshop East and on it goes. Talk to the local ACTRA office or Equity Advisory Council for information on what is going on in your city. Ask around. Use your networking skills.

A class is a place where you can fail and not worry. A good class is one where you are encouraged to take chances. You are there to learn, to grow, to experiment.

Classes and workshops not only exercise your body and mind, they also keep you in touch with the acting community even when you are out of work. We can all improve our skills and we all need to keep the rust off. If "being unemployed" for you means temping or teaching or waiting tables, it is easy to be ground down. Even if you're lucky, as we have been in recent years, and don't have to work outside the business, only performing readies you for performing. Gail Singer: "People who keep their juices flowing seem to have the work more easily accessible to them when it's required." Simply moving among fellow actors keeps the networks growing. You will not only learn skills at classes, you plug into opportunities to use the skills. And remember, the cost of any class is tax deductible if it helps you professionally.

OTHER PEOPLE'S WORK

Exercise for the mind: learning through watching. Get over the jealousy we all feel seeing someone else playing the part we "should" have got. (How many actors does it take to change a light bulb: ten. One to screw in the new bulb and nine to say, "I could do that.") Watching great performances can be an inspiration. Watching them analytically can be an education. The ordinary audience enjoys the excellent performance; the professional looks for the basic skills that make the performance excellent. August Schellenberg played Randolph in *Free Willy* as a complex human being, in what might have been merely an off-the-shelf producer-pleasing native Indian interpretation. Nicola Cavendish, in *Shirley Valentine*, the one-woman critical success, plays the central character and a dozen others so cleverly that it hardly looks like acting at all.

MAKING WORK

Any actor will tell you that the hardest part of an actor's work is being out of it. When you are employed, your energy is greater, your capacity to appreciate and enjoy life is increased and you generally function at a higher, more intense level of awareness. Being out of work brings with it anxiety, stress, depression and that awful feeling of having been found out. After all, if you were any good, you'd be working, right? Intellectually, we know that is rubbish but it haunts us all the same. The longer unemployment lasts, the more reinforced the belief becomes and the harder it is to lift yourself out of the mire of self-pity and boredom and into the stream of active participation in anything.

There may come a time when you have to be brave enough to pick up your skills and use them in a different area rather than become a perpetually unemployed actor groupie (see pages 155–56, "The Actor and Other Work"). Assuming you haven't come that far and that being an actor stills turns your crank, please break away from your sense of failure. Failure isn't missing the target; it's shooting yourself in the foot. As long as your publicity is going out and you give a good account of yourself at auditions, you're a success waiting to happen.

What can you do right now? The first thing is – anything! Just get off your butt and do something active to keep your energy up. Take a class, play squash, write letters, make phone calls, get in touch with your agent, read some new plays, work on your audition material, do some vocal exercises. There are dozens of ways to focus your mental and physical energy.

Create your own projects. If no one is offering you work, make your own. You don't need thousands of dollars to invest in an idea. Organize a showcase production with a group of like-minded actors. Develop a show for one of the Fringe Festivals. Perhaps you have watched a television show or listened to a radio drama and thought, "I could write one of those." Write one and submit it to the script consultant. These projects may not earn you any money but they will keep the creative juices flowing and people will see your work. In the case of a writing project, you may open up a whole new area.

Living Life

Your career is not your whole life. Concentrating solely on work destroys you not only as an actor but as a human being. Eva Brandstein, from *The Actor*: "Postponing your life until you 'make it' is one of the saddest decisions an actor can make. This is your life – now, right now. *This is not a rehearsal.*"

A career is not a substitute for family and friends. You should not put the people around you on hold. You need not give up music, politics, social issues, sports, philately, or soap-making for your career. Actors who are interested in nothing but acting are lifeless, boring and deadly – on-stage and off.

As people, we need a broad base of passion and interest to keep us fully alive. As actors, we need a rich, complex life from which to draw. Otherwise, our acting is a puny imitation of the real thing: watching an episode of "National Geographic" compared to visiting the Arctic.

You have to keep on at extending and improving yourself. All we have is what we are. If you feel good about yourself, you can handle all the unpredictables that professional life – and real life – will throw at you.

How does the real world affect the actor? See the next page.

Chapter Twelve
Grownups

"If you're old enough to be an actor,
you're old enough to know better."
– John Bjorgum

Young actors pride themselves on being outside the common herd. As the years go by, we continue to be outside but are no longer so happy about it. The *Applebaum-Hébert Report*: "[Artists strive to be different but] they want to be integrated into the society they live and work in. Social integration is the single most difficult problem an artist must face." Christopher Marston, executive director, Canadian Actors' Equity: "It's a tough life, not only because of psychological pressures of work and job-hunting, but also because of being outside the mainstream of society. It results in difficulties with establishing credit-worthiness because of job and residence impermanence and a varying income." Not fitting into the normal categories is romantic, until you are turned down for a credit card or a bank loan or a mortgage. Then those dull, pedestrian categories start looking pretty good. How can actors reconcile an artistically satisfying profession with the "real" world?

THE ACTOR AND A PERSONAL LIFE
Everyone needs the support and understanding of loving friends and family. Actors often get neither. Even when your nearest and dearest support you, it is rare that they understand you or what you do. Parents are always delighted when you get work, even if it's not a "real job," but can't understand why you won't leave the set a couple of hours early to attend your favourite cousin's wedding.

In one-to-one relationships, actors have a notoriously bad track record. (We have to decide what we are going to call the person in your life. "Spouse" limits it to married people. "Significant other" makes us gag. "Friend" is coy. Let's go with "mate." It has a married connotation but also the British meaning of "pal." If you can think of a better word, please let us know. We'll use it in the next edition.) We don't have actual statistics but from looking around at people in the business, we see that long-term relationships are the exception, not the rule. Certainly, actors have no less desire for a steady, loving pairing than the rest of the world. Why, then, is it so difficult for them to succeed?

Separation is a major pressure. Most actors go where the work is. In the authors' first three years "together," we were apart for a total of eighteen months. However, separation in itself is not the problem. There are airline personnel and travelling salesmen and truck drivers whose relationships are able to withstand the distances. But combine physical separation with an intense working relationship and you have the formula for trouble.

A group of people, many of whom are total strangers, act out the most personal, intimate and emotional moments in human experience. Working associates who were introduced yesterday watch and offer comments as you expose the tenderest and most vulnerable parts of your psyche. Just another day down at the acting factory. To deal with this situation, you quickly develop a group identity and loyalty with bonds as strong as those in the most tightly-knit family. In fact, "family" is a word actors frequently use to describe their working team. When this feeling is combined with the absence of your mate, the sense of separation is vast.

Actors can find it difficult to separate the professional and the personal. Before you become more experienced in the ritual of meetings and leave-takings, it is easy to believe that your group will remain close and special friends long after the final curtain or the wrap party. It won't. Work relationships have a limited shelf life but while you are working, they can be extraordinarily close and that closeness can endanger more important relationships. ("Tell me, Sir Henry, did Hamlet ever sleep with Ophelia?" "Always in my companies, dear boy, always.") On-stage love and lust can easily carry off stage. The emotions are real and intense but rarely long-lasting. In the process of finding that out, people get hurt. Be aware that there is a danger of damaging a long-term relationship because you cannot recognize the boundaries of a professional one.

Having a mate in the business has advantages. At least your mate will understand what you are going through when the audition you did was lousy or the engagers decided to cast a "known quantity" or the writer changed the sex of the part. Not necessarily. Professional jealousy is a fact of life. We know it is ridiculous to be angry when your mate gets an audition or a job offer and you don't. It is unlikely, even if you are a gay couple, that you would be up for the same part but knowing that doesn't help much. Early on in the authors' relationship, jealousy was a big problem. Whether we are wiser now, or just older and tireder, we realize what a waste of energy it is.

Work is involving. So is unemployment. If you are depressed about being out of work and your beloved is complaining about billing on the contract, you are going to find it hard to summon up much compassion. Even when you are both working, your fascination with your own work makes it difficult to open up to your mate's. When you are both out of work, a whole new set of tensions enter the equation. One of you is "up" and doing the *rounds* and the other has hit a bad slump and deeply resents any activity more positive than turning over in bed. All you can do is reach out to the other person. Self-absorption is death.

Having a long-term mate outside the business should make life easier. Another source of income, a different schedule, a different set of priorities so that things stay in proportion. But it's not all good. Few people outside the profession can appreciate the stress and worry, the highs and lows that are our daily companions. However sympathetic and understanding your non-actor partner tries to be, you find it easier to communicate with actor friends, people who've been there. Your partner feels isolated, not allowed into one of the most important parts of your world.

Sometimes an actor pairs well with a stage manager or a technician. The competition and jealousy are reduced (but not removed) and the sympathy is increased by knowing some of the problems first hand.

THE ACTOR AND OTHER WORK

Most actors do more than act. They have to, if they want to eat. Early in your career the necessity for secondary employment is a fact of life. What sort of job do you want? How do you go about finding it?

Secondary employment can be a touchy subject. Some actors hate to admit they need to work outside the profession. Somehow it smacks of failure. Rubbish. It would be wonderful if your acting income alone could support you but in all likelihood it won't. StatsCan tells us that, among professionally active actors, around half make some money from a job outside the business, half get money from a non-acting job in the business and a quarter have a regular full- or part-time job. Don't be ashamed to acknowledge your second job. It is allowing you some freedom from financial anxiety and the ability to concentrate on your profession rather than on your survival.

The other job you do doesn't have to be secondary. Genie Award-winning actor Thomas Peacocke happily admits that his main profession and great love is teaching (he is in the Department of Drama at the University of Alberta). That does not stop him from performing on stage and in film and television. You don't have to swear an oath to put acting first. You decide. It's your life.

Most people, though, think of other jobs as a way of supporting their acting habit. The standard secondary jobs for actors are those which allow flexible hours for auditions: temp work, telephone marketing, bartending, waiting tables, house-cleaning, painting, renovating. Work is available in these areas all the time. Find a job that suits you and show that you're reliable so you can go back when you need it again.

Although it is easy enough to phone up a temp agency or answer an ad for telephone marketing, the way to find secondary employment is to use your networking skills. Fellow-actors are your best bet. They know the employers who positively like actors and are really prepared for your being off to audition at a moment's notice. ACTRA and Equity have secondary job information and companies occasionally advertise in the Equity newsletter.

Do you want a job totally outside the profession or one connected with it? An outside job is likely to be better paid but an inside job keeps you in touch. The authors' teaching, private coaching and writing do not pay hugely but we remain part of the acting community.

Your second job may become more important and consuming than your acting. There is no rule that says you can't change your mind. If your second job gives you an excitement, an interest or a security that you need and want and that you do not get from acting, go for it. Why not? Leaving acting and taking up beekeeping full time is not an admission of failure. It is a mature decision arrived at after careful thought.

Or it should be. Don't let a particularly bad bout of unemployment get you so depressed that you throw your career over in a fit of despair. Sit down and assess your situation. If the acting minuses now outweigh the acting pluses, it may be time for a change. Pack up your skills and knowledge and experience, and use them elsewhere. No decision is irreversible. You may want to try something else for a while and come back to acting later on with a whole new set of experiences to enrich your work. If you don't come back, that's all right, too.

THE ACTOR AND THE ESTABLISHMENT

Actors are stuck with the "rogues and vagabonds" myth. No matter how grownup our behaviour is in private or public, we suffer from society's view that we are not quite trustworthy. Some of our bad press is justified. Most of us are poor and nomadic – not something designed to endear you to the local bank manager. However, much of our bad press comes from ignorance and misrepresentation. The general public reads the *National Enquirer*, not the Equity newsletter.

Norman Bethune said: "An artist makes uneasy the static, the set and the still." Members of the Establishment don't like us. We don't fit on their forms. Society is run for the benefit of the average, so we are bound to have some problems. We can only fight their misconceptions by being as Establishment as we can. When dealing with a bureaucrat, dress the part. Pretend it's an audition for the role of a business executive. You will create a much better impression if you – what is the expression? – "dress for success."

Treat the bureaucrats as people and they may return the compliment. If they don't, it is always possible to go higher. "We are having a problem dealing with this," you might say, "I wonder if I could talk to your supervisor?" Shoving your file down the clerk's throat is more satisfying but only in the short term.

Get all your facts together before you face one of these people. Make life easier for them. Don't attempt to write last year's eight engagers in that little space on the form. Probably all they want is "self-employed" and your income, near enough. If you have had as many apartments as job rejections, use your parents' address. Filling in these forms is like writing a résumé or having a job interview. Avoid lies but put the best face on things you can from their point of view.

When dealing with banks, department stores and credit organizations, you enter your gross income. However, it is not your income that is the main concern. Anyone lending you money wants an assurance that they will get it back. You need a credit rating and to get a credit rating, you need a credit rating. Catch 22? Not necessarily. Just prove that you are an excellent debtor. (Unfortunately a student loan doesn't count.) Take out a small bank loan secured with an equal amount frozen in a term certificate. Be frank with your bank manager why you want this. Pay it back on schedule. Bingo, you've proved you can handle credit responsibly. It will cost you the difference in interest rates between the term certificate and the personal loan, so keep the term down to six months or so. You could swallow your pride and run a credit card with a parent as co-signer. It's a good first step to getting your own card with the same company.

Is it necessary to establish credit? Maybe not, but try hiring a car with cash. What do you do when you get to the airport and find that the prepaid ticket you negotiated hasn't been prepaid? A credit card can be very useful in an emergency.

House and apartment contents insurance rates are slightly higher for actors. Quite reasonably. Insurers love couch potatoes who go away once a year and have a non-smoking, teetotal accountant look after the place while they are gone. The best we can do is to ask different insurance brokers to quote for the same coverage and find the company that gives us the best rates.

THE ACTOR AND THE GOVERNMENT

Grants

Keith Digby, freelance director: "Grant-getting is honourable. Not trying to get a grant for which you are qualified is self-inflicted poverty." It isn't necessary to struggle all on your own. Canada does show some awareness of the artist's worth to society. Across the country, there are grant-giving bodies designed to help people in the arts. The largest, most comprehensive of these bodies is the Canada Council, which is under the umbrella of the federal government. To be eligible as an actor for a theatre grant, you must have two years' experience with professional companies and be either a Canadian citizen or have five years' landed immigrant status. You may not have two grants simultaneously from the Canada Council, although you may have money from other sources for the same project. The grants include:

Arts Grants B These are "intended to help artists to do personal creative work or to improve their skills."

You get travel costs and living costs to a maximum of around fifteen thousand dollars, including project costs.

Renewals are possible with further application. The juries rarely recommend more than two consecutive grants.

You may apply only once in twelve months. If unsuccessful, you may apply for a Project Grant or a Travel Grant but for a different project.

Project Grants These grants may be used for living expenses and/or project costs, depending on your needs.

You may apply only once in twelve months.

Travel Grants Travel grants are to "enable artists to travel on occasions important to their professional careers" (working under eminent artist-teachers, taking an active part in national and international meetings).

You get excursion air fare from your place of residence to the destination and a *per diem* of twenty dollars for a maximum of five days.

You are allowed one every twelve months unless you have had a travel allowance with a Project Grant in the preceding twelve months.

Explorations This programme is for those who don't seem to fit in any other programme. It "encourages innovative projects by individuals, groups and organizations in Canada which may introduce new approaches to creative expression, cross disciplines or fulfil specific needs in the development of the arts."

The Canada Council publishes a brochure, *Aid to Artists*, which is revised yearly (mailing address on page 194).

Every province has grant-giving agencies. Write to your local arts council (see Addresses, page 194) to find out what sort of grants your province provides. If the money is there, you might as well be the one to receive it. Your provincial arts and culture department may know about city grants and local, private grant-giving foundations, as well. Six provinces that we know of publish booklets or newsletters that may give you useful local knowledge.

Provincial Health Care Plans

Each province has its own health insurance scheme, with its own rules and regulations, but any province that charges premiums has a Premium Assistance scheme. This is a provision for lowering (sometimes to zero) premiums for low-income subscribers. That's us, folks. Their form asks for last year's income and your projection for this year. Some provinces ask for proof, in which case a copy of the front page of your income tax return should do the trick. Don't bother to explain the impossibility of the projection of future earnings. Just put in a reasonable figure.

Income Tax

There, we've said it. That wasn't so bad, was it? And neither, believe us, is filling in a tax form. If you have been conscientious throughout the year, income tax is a breeze. If you haven't been, it's more of a Force 9 gale. It only gets worse if you put it off; Revenue Canada loves to jump up and down on people who don't file, even if the tax in question is laughably small.

Audit. There are actors who can't say the word without breaking out in hives. In fact, Revenue Canada can't possibly check everyone's return so they look over the arithmetic, run some cross-checks and pass you for now. Then they pick a group or two – every sheet metal worker in St. John's, Newfoundland, thirty-five-year-olds with more than six children, fat bearded gentlemen in the reindeer business – and examine their returns in more detail. They are not accusing you of anything, they just want to see the evidence for what you claimed. If you have at least tried to keep good records, you needn't fear. But if you are audited, you may want to spend a chunk of money on an accountant to go over your records and get you prepared, even if you plan on going into the lion's den alone.

As an actor, union or not, you are self-employed, unless you work in Newfoundland. If you do other work as well, you may also be an employee. The tax form has places to enter both sets of income.

When you are an employee, your employer is legally obliged to deduct tax from your pay before you get it, along with CPP and UIC payments. Once you have about fifteen weeks of UIC payments, you can claim UIC benefits.

As a self-employed person, you don't need to have tax deducted from your pay. If you earn enough to have $1,000 of federal tax due, the tax man will send you a note telling you to pay next year's tax in quarterly instalments. Not a major problem for most of us. You have to pay your own CPP with no contribution from your engagers and you may not have UIC deducted, nor can you claim UIC benefits based on your acting work. (Canada is the only country we have found world-wide where acting income doesn't qualify you for unemployment benefits.)

The union newsletters have tax columns for performers: Equity, once a year, and ACTRA in Toronto, with four shorter columns, once a quarter. You may also find our *Canadian Performers' Tax Kit* useful (available from Theatrebooks, see page 200, or from us). With those aids and the rest of this chapter you should sail through tax time efficiently and painlessly.

Keep records of everything, incoming and outgoing. Keep a diary of all your professional appointments and engagements. Keep receipts of all your purchases. Keep pay slips from all your jobs. Although you will be submitting to Revenue Canada only the few receipts they actually request, you must have available, in case of an audit, evidence of every single outgoing expense and incoming fee.

How you keep your records is up to you. The authors use their own *Canadian Performers' Tax Kit* (of course). You can use any stationery store system you like or have around. Cheaper than prepackaged accordion files, but less convenient, are big envelopes, labelled and punched and put into a three-ring binder. If you want to fill a pillow case all year long and sort the receipts out at the end of the year, that is up to you. Whatever works best. (We do not recommend the pillow case method, ourselves, but then we're just a couple of old fuddy-duddies.)

The ideal receipt has on it the name and address of the store, your name and address, the date, the purchase, the amount, how it was paid (cash, Visa, etc.), and the salesperson's initials. Under $30, say, ordinary cash-register receipts are all right. Scribble "$12.75 make-up" on the receipt right away and you won't have a pocket full of anonymous litter when you get around to clearing it out.

You may not dump your tax information even after you have received an OK from Revenue Canada. Books and records must be retained for six years from the end of the last taxation year to which they relate. If you want to destroy them any earlier you must get written permission. Revenue Canada can audit four years back, more if they suspect fraud. After six years, breathe a sigh of relief and chuck it.

Around February or March, your employers and engagers should send you official tax statements for all the money they paid you. In reality, they may not. But with or without an official statement, you have to declare all your income. Send in the statements you have received and attach a list of all your income for the year. (See page 168.) Your acting income is on a T4A statement, any employed income is on a T4 statement and investment income, including bank interest, is on a T5 statement. (Banks don't have to send out T5's unless your interest comes to over a hundred dollars but you still have to declare it.) Make sure the engager has used the right form.

Now comes the fun part. Deductible expenses. The basic rule is you deduct anything you spent with the intention of getting work. You will be astonished and delighted at what you are allowed to deduct, as long as the items are properly receipted. (Speaking of receipts, we might as well give you some acceptable unreceipted expenses: quarters for business calls on pay phones, bus or subway fare and money for parking meters for business travel. You enter all these expenses in your professional appointments diary. It may seem a petty amount to worry about – a quarter for a phone call – but it is amazing how quickly those quarters add up.)

The following headings are the ones we use. It really doesn't matter as long as it seems logical and you don't keep changing your classifications.

Advertising and Promotion: résumés, photographs, subscription to artists' directory, voice tapes, videotapes.

Entertainment: The latest interpretation allows you to claim 80% of "a reasonable amount … for food, beverages or entertainment incurred in earning income." For example, you can entertain directors you want to work for, actors you're working with, writers who will tell you about their new play. Why 80%? The logical tax people say you'd be eating anyway, wouldn't you? Make a note of the conversation in your work diary to show it was a professional expense. Include any home entertainment – keep all those supermarket receipts and liquor bills.

Agent Commission: the whole shmear.

Bank Charges: only if you have a business account.

Car: not nearly as tricky as some people think. Calculate what percentage of your yearly mileage is business use. Claim that percentage of your total operating expenses. What expenses can you claim? Everything: gas, oil, servicing, insurance, licence, motor league, repairs. How do you decide what percentage to use? Keep a log book in the car. Enter the mileage on January 1, then write down the beginning and end mileage of each business trip and what you did – photocopied a résumé, went to a class. Enter your mileage on December 31, get out your handy-dandy calculator, add up all the business miles and work that out as a percentage of the total miles you have driven.

Because your home is your main base of operations, unless you have an office elsewhere, any trip for a business purpose is deductible. Otherwise, your trips from home to work and back are not deductible.

Dressing Room Supplies: anything you use for a performance. Not only make-up and make-up towels, but deodorant, Kleenex, contact lens solution, hair spray, tampons, soap, shampoo, etc. But it's no fair carrying your toothpaste back and forth to use at home. It has to be used only in the dressing room.

Hair: styling and cut for a specific role – 100 percent.

General styling – be reasonable about it. Our appearance and its maintenance is part of our job, so some expense is allowable.

Local Transportation: Claim the taxi if it was necessary, use bus transfers as receipts. Ask for a receipt for your transit pass or bulk tokens, and claim a business proportion.

Office Space: If you have a separate space devoted to office or work use (and it must be more than a corner of your kitchen table), you may write off a portion of your living expenses – rent, utilities, mortgage interest, insurance, etc. This may reduce your provincial tax credits.

Office Supplies: tape, pens, typewriter ribbons or cassettes, staples, address stamps, hole punch, liquid paper, calculator, erasers, etc. Large equipment like typewriter or word processor will go under Capital Cost Allowance (see below).

Out of Town: Living away from home costs extra and you can deduct the extra expense. Claim all your out-of-town rent or hotel costs if you are keeping on your in-town base. Of course, if you sublet your home apartment, the tax man will expect you to declare as income the rent you get. Of course. Remember, you're not living at home so taxis are more freely allowable. You'll eat out more. Keep all your food and restaurant receipts and claim whatever portion you think is over your at-home costs. As our friendly local tax man says, "You'd have to eat at home, too."

Don't believe anyone who says Revenue Canada allows you an out-of-town *per diem* without receipts. *Not true.* You may get away with claiming twenty dollars for each out of town day but, when you're audited, you won't be allowed a penny of it without receipts.

Postage and Stationery: Get receipts. It's more convenient to buy stamps in bulk. But you can get a receipt for a single stamp.

Professional Development: It used to be that only the cost of coaching for a specific role was deductible. Now it is possible to deduct the general coaching that keeps us tuned as artists (singing classes, professional workshops but not the Y).

Claim for books, plays, accent tapes, etc., and any research expenses.

Professional Dues: Equity, ACTRA, UDA, etc. Only the yearly dues, not the initiation fee. Do not deduct these from your gross professional income. They have a special slot on the tax form: "Step 3 – Calculation of Taxable Income. Annual union, professional or the like dues." (Initiation fees are Eligible Capital Expenditures – look at your Business and Professional Income Tax Guide.)

Professional Gifts: first night cards, telegrams, flowers, booze.

Professional Journals: all journals, periodicals, magazines and publications, as long as they are work-related. You can deduct part of the cost of magazines and newspapers that are not wholly related to your career but have arts sections or theatre and film reviews.

Professional Tickets: any play or film you attend and by extension, any concert, opera or ballet. Not football; not Jello-wrestling.

Telephone: Deduct 100 percent of business long-distance calls. If you have a business line, claim the whole shot. Otherwise, you may claim Call Answer (voice mail). We haven't received a ruling on Call Waiting or Call Forwarding. You might make a case for claiming a business proportion of those services but we don't guarantee it.

Travel: all your travel costs to an out-of-town job but only if your engager isn't obliged to pay your fare. If your engager is obliged to pay but doesn't, you still can't claim it, even though you paid it. Lousy, but true.

Wardrobe: only the percentage that is used for work. Any large item (over $100) should come under laundry, dry cleaning.

Capital Cost Allowance: If you buy any item of "enduring" value – computer, oboe, car, suit – you can't deduct the whole cost in the year you bought it. You can claim CCA, a percentage of the cost, in any year you continue to own it. You have to fill in the CCA form in the Revenue Canada Business and Professional Guide, which gives you all the information you need and more.

Don't worry if your expenses exceed your acting income. Just enter a negative net professional income. When you add up all your income (net self-employed, employed and investment), your negative acting income will reduce the total. In effect, your secondary income is helping to pay your acting expenses. The tax man will look oddly at you if you claim to have lived for a year on a net income of $417, unless you can show outstanding loans or withdrawal from savings.

A good way to reduce your taxable income is to buy a Retirement Savings Plan. Revenue Canada tells you how much RRSP contribution you can deduct from this year's taxable income when it sends you the Notice of Assessment of last year's tax return. Paying no tax now, and none on the interest as it builds up, can really help. A thousand dollars in an RRSP, assuming only an 8% return, will give you $23,400 in forty years time. That thousand in a bank will give you only $9,500 to retire on. Spend it on scuba gear and you'll have nothing at all, of course.

That's pretty well everything. If you have investment income, you fill in Schedule 5. If you've had open heart surgery and a root canal, you fill in Schedule 4.

With enough patience, a calculator and a stiff scotch, anyone can work through a tax return. However, if this chapter is making you queasy, you can get your tax done for you for $200 and up. Way up. You'll save money if you use this chapter to get things organised ahead of time. Most accountants and tax preparers know nothing about an actor's specific problems, so ask around for someone knowledgeable. Call us (416-960-1785) and we'll do your tax at a cut rate. Remember, you remain legally responsible for your return, so be sure you understand what has been done on your behalf.

GST

You don't have to register if your self-employed income is less than about $28,000, but if you do, you'll get back all the GST you pay on your expenses.

After you register, you charge your engagers GST, an extra 7 percent of your gross self-employed income, and file a GST return quarterly or annually. The return asks for four figures: your professional income, the GST on it, your expenses, the GST on them. You pass on to Revenue Canada Excise the GST you were paid, minus the GST you paid the stores, which can amount to a substantial savings. You'll save even more by opting to use the Quick Method, if your expenses are relatively low. Simply send Canada Excise

4 percent of your total income up to $30,000 (5 percent on any over $30,000).

Once registered, don't include the GST in your expenses for income tax.

Final Warning: Don't believe your friends. Don't believe your accountant. Don't believe us. Revenue Canada, Taxation and Excise, will send you full information. Call them. It's *your* money, *you* sign the form. It's *you* they will audit – and it's you who will have to pay for the mistakes you let someone else make for you.

EDITH EGGAR
192 32nd Street
Vancouver, B.C.
V9Z 1H8
(604) 555-7856

EXPENSES 1993

SOCIAL INSURANCE NUMBER: 488 596 544

Advertising and Promotion (includes entertainment)	$ 1,123.45
Agent Commission	1,142.99
Bank Charges	7.876
Car (1,607 x 48%)	771.76
Dressing Room Supplies	97.78
Hair	58.00
Office Supplies	166.59
Out of Town Expenses	1,248.73
Postage and Stationary	340.58
Professional Development	142.15
Professional Gifts	340.58
Professional Journals	70.54
Professional Tickets	97.00
Telephone (includes answering service)	1,135.49
Travel	433.35
Wardrobe	184.95
Capital Cost Allowance	62.93
TOTAL	$ 7,290.60

EDITH EGGAR

192 32nd Street
Vancouver, B.C.
V9Z 1H8
(604) 555-7856

INCOME 1993
SOCIAL INSURANCE NUMBER: 488 596 544

SELF-EMPLOYED INCOME:

StageWest, Edmonton	$ 6,060.00
Belfry Theatre, Victoria	3,456.12
CBC	614.00
TV Ontario	13.58
Performer Payroll Services, Inc.	867.32
Talent and Residuals, Inc.	1,577.90
TOTAL	$ 12,588.92

EMPLOYED INCOME:

Office Assistance	3,127.44
Humber College	956.51
TOTAL	$ 4,083.95

INVESTMENT INCOME:

National Trust	311.92
CIBC Interest	110.31
TOTAL	$ 422.23

Envoi

"It's a good answer which knows how to stop."
– Italian proverb

We could go on forever. Each time we start to write "The End," we remember another problem you're bound to face or another question you're likely to ask. However, if this book is to remain not only easy to read but also easy to carry, it is time to call a halt. Besides, if there are no surprises in store, why enter into this glorious, absurd adventure?

"The wise man learns by example, the fool by experience." There has got to be a bit of the fool in any actor, so we willingly allow you to make your own mistakes and learn by them. Perhaps *you* will be writing the sequel to this.

In the meantime, we wish you luck, guts and good management.

Glossary

Terms in SMALL CAPITALS are also listed as separate items.

Actor-proof	The play will work, however bad the acting. The prop cannot be broken by an actor.
AD	(1) In theatre: ARTISTIC DIRECTOR.
	(2) In film or TV: assistant director. First AD can be an executive position, second AD, third AD, etc., do whatever non-technical jobs need doing.
ADR	Automatic dialogue replacement. In POST-PRODUCTION, taping lines, new or already recorded in the shooting, to fit the existing visuals. Also called looping.
Advance	(1) Casual sales, not subscription tickets, bought before the day of performance or before a touring company arrives to play an engagement. (2) Salary paid before it is due.
AEA	Actors' Equity Association. American stage union.
AFTRA	American Federation of Television and Radio Artists.
Agency	(1) Actors' agent's office and company.
	(2) The advertising agency which devises a commercial and then hires a PRODUCTION COMPANY to make it.
Alternative	(of theatre companies) Not in the mainstream. Politically and/or artistically progressive.

Ambience   (1) Media slang for haze produced by smoke machine.
(2) Media term for subliminal sound plus acoustics of "silent" set.

Apron   In PROSCENIUM theatre, stage area downstage of the proscenium arch.

Arena Stage   Theatre in the round. The audience is on all sides.

Artistic Director   Head of theatre organization. Decides plays and guest directors, casts and directs plays, deals with crises, is responsible for artistic policy.

ASM   Assistant stage manager. Without whom theatre would die.

Available   (1) Of light: natural light or regular indoor lights, unaugmented by film or television lighting.
(2) Of an actor: not working.

Back Light   In media THREE-POINT LIGHTING, the light shining on the far side of a person, to lift them from the background.

Barn Doors   Opaque panels hinged at the sides of a lighting instrument, to block off the edges of the beam of light. Shutters.

Batten   (1) Pipe to which lights and scenery are attached in order to be flown.
(2) Wood, often 2-by-4, used to weight the bottom of a soft flying piece.

Best Boy   Chief assistant to the head GAFFER. "Best-boy grip" does the same for the KEY GRIP.

BG   Background. Media jargon.

Big Close-up   BCU. A tight shot. The face fills the screen.

Billing   Definition of where, how and when one's name is to be used in advertising a show.

Bit Part   Small role, especially in media. He does a bit part, your role is interesting, I have a cameo appearance.

Blacks   ("Soft blacks") Black drapes hung to hide part of backstage.

Blow   Forget one's lines, ruin a crucial moment.

Book   Script. The spoken words, not the lyrics, of a musical.

Book Show   A musical with a plot.

Boom   The long arm which places the microphone close to the actor but off camera. Generally.

Box Office   (1) Ticket-selling department.
                     (2) The gross takings from ticket sales.

Breakdown   Details of the characters the CASTING DIRECTOR is trying to cast. Sent to agents for suggestions from their rosters.

Bus and   A production touring to second-class dates, the
Truck Company   company and costumes in a bus, the scenery in trucks.

Business   (1) The entertainment or performing arts industries.
                     (2) A series of actions, often comic, e.g. setting table, lighting cigarette, falling on bum. "Great bit of business, dear! Never do it again!" (Often abbreviated to "biz" in either sense.)

Buy-out   Allows a media ENGAGER to pay, up front, at a discount, for various future uses of a programme.

Call   The time your ENGAGER wants your services. Wardrobe call, half hour call, train call, etc.

Call Board Bulletin board where theatre calls and company and union messages are posted.

Call-back A second or later audition for the same job. Theoretically the odds improve as call-backs multiply.

Cameo Small part with big potential for being noticed. Any small part played by a big actor.

Cart Audio cartridge, cassette tape.

Casting Couch Sexual harassment of actresses. And actors.

Casting Agency Hired by an ENGAGER in smaller centres to provide actors from those on the agency's books for auditions for a project. Paid by the engager, not by the actors.

Casting Director Hired by a media production company to suggest actors who will be auditioned. Sends out BREAKDOWNS to agents, who submit suitable actors' names.

Cheating Appearing to look at one's fellow actor but actually facing slightly downstage (or toward the camera) to enable the audience to see one's face or actions better.

Chew the Scenery Overact, ham it up.

Clapper Board (SLATE) A small blackboard, or high-tech equivalent, on which is recorded, at the beginning of each shot, details of the shot to identify the film or tape later in the editing room.

Clapper Loader The AD who fills in the slate, and who often also loads the camera with film.

Client (1) Company whose products are being advertised.
(2) An actor on an agent's ROSTER.

Close-up   CU. A head (and shoulders) shot.

Cloth   Painted canvas flying piece with BATTENS top and bottom.

Cold Reading   An audition with little or no time to work on the script.

Commercial Theatre   Supported by ticket sales alone, with no grants or donations.

Comp   "Complimentary ticket." Free ticket or pass given to the cast for guests. See PAPER.

Company Manager   (1) On tour, the theatre's representative. Deals with transport, accommodation, salaries and much, much more.
(2) In large resident theatres, similar to PSM.

Concession   Part of the normal union contract may be set aside by the union to make a deserving engager's life easier. Hrrmph.

Continuity   Especially in out-of-sequence film shooting, matching the positions, colours, etc. of things at the end of a shot with the same things at the beginning of the next shot.
Person responsible for such matching.

Costumes   Clothes worn by the actors. Clothes carried but not worn are PROPS. Clothes on the set but not carried or worn are DRESSING. The basis of many a craft union problem.

Cover Shot   A SAFETY. An extra taken after a good take, "just in case."
Occasionally = MASTER SHOT.

Crab   Of a camera: to move across the action, e.g., along the baseline of a tennis game while looking at the net.

Craft Services   The job, and hence the people doing it, of providing snacks and coffee on a set.

Credit   (1) A part played, appearing on a résumé.
(2) BILLING, in the media.

Crossing the Line   Shooting the action from different sides. Confusing and to be avoided.

CTA   Canadian Theatre Agreement.

Cue Light   The most common visual cue. Can be "red, warn," "green, go" or "on, warn," "off, go."

Curtain   On any stage, the end of the show. From traditional PROSCENIUM theatre.

Cut   (1) Stop filming the action.
(2) Change instantly from one shot to another.
(3) To edit.
(4) To take out (dialogue, your best scene, etc.).

Cyclorama   Cyc (pronounced "sike"). Curved surface of cloth or cement, round the entire back of the stage or set, on which sky effects and slides can be projected.

Dance Captain   Often a senior chorus member, who maintains the choreography during the run and often acts as assistant choreographer through rehearsals.

Dark   Describes a theatre with no show in performance.

Dead   Of any space, having no echo at all.

Defer   Contractual agreement to delay part of a fee until the project has started to make some money.

Demo (Demo tape) Videotape with five to eight minutes of representative media work, to send to potential engagers. See Chapter Four, "Show and Tell."

Deputy Elected member of a theatre cast who maintains liaison between Equity and the management.

Director of Photography (DOP, Cinematographer) Supervises the lighting and camera style in TV or film shooting. May also operate camera ("lighting cameraman").

DLP Dead-letter perfect. Knowing all one's lines. "I was DLP on the bus but now it's gone."

Dolly Wheeled platform for camera. "Dolly in/out," to follow the action by moving the camera.

Dormancy When a commercial is being shown on TV, the actor may not work for another similar product. A dormancy fee extends this prohibition over a period when the advert is temporarily off the air.

Dramaturge One who recommends plays to the AD of a theatre and works with playwrights on new scripts.

Dresser In theatre, a person, often from maintenance WARDROBE, who helps actors into and out of costume.

Dressing Object on the set for its appearance only, not for use.

Drop Canvas or fabric flown piece without rigid framework.

Dub (1) In video, to make a copy of a tape, such a copy.
(2) To record new sound, e.g., English over original Urdu.

Edit	Put film or TV shots or radio segments together to form the final product.
Effects	FX. Technical tricks, sight or sound, to enhance a production.
Eighty-Six	To cut, turn off, stop using, dispose of something. The alleged reason for the expression is worth asking about.
Engagement	A paying acting job.
Engager	In media work, a person or company which hires and pays actors.
Ensemble	A cast working as equals. Sometimes including the stars.
Establishing Shot	Sets up the situation for the audience. Snow falls: it's winter. Big Ben rings over a street with carriages: it's Victorian London.
Executive Producer	In film, above the producer, although sometimes only as a name to attract backing.
Extraordinary Risk	Equity demands that hazardous work (what in media might be called a stunt) be contracted as such and receive better-than-usual insurance coverage.
Extreme Close-up	ECU. Shot showing eyes to mouth or less.
Eye Line	In media, where someone is looking. Conventionally, heroes look slightly down when talking to women.
Fake	(1) Ad lib, having forgotten something. (2) Give a sufficient impression of doing something (writing a letter, cutting off your children's heads) which would in reality take too long or otherwise be awkward.

Feature   Film made to be shown in cinemas.

Featured   Prominently billed under the first billing.

Fill Light   In media THREE-POINT LIGHTING, throws light into the shadows caused by the KEY LIGHT.

Flag   Panel held or on a stand; translucent to soften the light or opaque to cut the spread of light. Cf. BARN DOORS.

Flat   A piece of scenery, usually rectangular, four to eight feet wide. Traditionally a wooden frame covered with canvas but now, following TV's lead, often masonite-covered.

Floor   The film or TV studio itself, not the control room.

Fly   To raise scenery by ropes. "The flies": Space above the stage where such scenery hangs; "Flying piece": scenery flown as a unit.

Focus Puller   Watches the action and changes the camera's focus to preset marks as the actor moves.

FOH   Front of house. The audience part of a theatre, and its staff.

Foley Artist   Adds sound to recorded scenes, in POST-PRODUCTION, to replace or enhance existing sound like footsteps, locks, fight noises.

Frame   The imaginary line around what the camera can see. "In frame," "out of frame," "frame it tight."

Freelance   Not on a staff contract. Brought in for a specific job.

Fringe   (F. theatre, f. festival) Experimental, ALTERNATIVE theatre. From the Edinburgh Fringe Festival, where such productions are mounted around the main Festival of more Establishment works.

Full House	No seats available. Except for the BOX OFFICE's little pets.
FX	Effects. Lighting or sound (SFX).
Gaffer Tape	Two-inch-wide adhesive cloth tape, like duct tape, without which media and theatre production would founder.
Gaffer	Media head electrician, responsible for lights, etc.
Gel	Transparent coloured sheet put in front of a lighting instrument. From "gelatin," now replaced by scorch-proof plastic.
General Manager	Administrative boss of theatre. Over office, box-office and custodial staff. Nominally under ARTISTIC DIRECTOR. Negotiates actors' contracts.
Get-in	The process of moving a touring set, costumes and properties from the trucks to the stage for the coming performance.
Glossy	Actor's eight-by-ten-inch publicity photograph.
Gobo	Perforated opaque screen inserted in the focal plane of a lamp to cast shadows of, e.g., tree branches on the stage.
Grease Paint	Still means stage make-up generically but in fact it's now more often lighter water-based pancake make-up as used on TV and in the street.
Grid	Gridiron. Beams over the stage, carrying the pulleys of the flying system.
Grievance	Formal complaint filed by a union against an engager. The first stage in the arbitration procedure.

Grip   Media carpenters and roustabouts. Head is KEY GRIP.

Guest Artist   Equity members may work for non-union companies only by permission under a GA contract.

Head Shot   Actor's eight-by-ten-inch publicity photograph.

Hold the Book   To prompt, especially when running lines.

Honey Wagon   Trailer divided into make-up and dressing cubicles. Each has its own separate lavatory facilities. Hence the name?

House   The audience, and also the auditorium. "Open the h." – allow the audience in.

House Seats   A theatre will often not sell certain good seats until the last minute, to be able to offer them as a courtesy to professional visitors.

Industrial   (1) Stage show for dealers and salesmen, entertaining the audience and extolling the product. A modern medicine show.
(2) Television production for in-house use, for training or morale.

Industry   The acting business, particularly the film part of it.

Ingenue   Pretty young actress who plays innocents. Such a part, e.g., Cecily in *The Importance of Being Earnest*.

In-House   (1) Not intended to be seen by anyone other than the engagers' client's employees.
(2) Done by someone in a permanent staff position.

Iron   Fireproof curtain lowered at the front of a PROSCENIUM stage in case of fire, to cut the actors off from the audience, exiting in safety.

Jobbed-in	A free lance has been hired to do the specific job.
Jurisdiction	The particular range of work and the particular geographical area a union has responsibility for and power over.
Juvenile Lead	Male ingenue, e.g., Nick in *Who's Afraid of Virginia Woolf?*
Key Light	In media: provides highlights on actor's face.
Key Grip	Head of department doing moving and building on media set.
Klieg Light	An early trade name (from Herr Kliegl, the inventor) for a carbon arc light.
Late Payment	When media fees aren't paid on time, this is the union-prescribed penalty fee. Sometimes collected.
Lavalier	Small condenser microphone pinned on or hung around neck.
Lazzi	Commedia del Arte term for a standard piece of business.
Left	Stage left: actor's left, facing the audience. Camera left: actor's right, facing the camera.
Legs	Narrow drapes at the side of the stage, masking the wings from the audience's view.
Libretto	Book, or text, of a musical comedy.
Lime (Light)	Powerful movable spotlight. Now normally an electric arc light.
Live	(1) Not recorded. (2) Carrying electricity. (3) Of a studio, etc., full of echo.

Live on Tape	(Live to tape) Recorded and then shown without editing, as if it were being transmitted live.
Local Jobber	Someone who is not, never has been and does not want to be a professional actor, who signs an affidavit to that effect and is hired by an Equity theatre as part of the "nonprofessional" quota.
Long Shot	(LS) The picture shows a full-length standing figure, up to a full landscape.
LX	Electrics.
Looping	POST-SYNCHING.
Management	Theatre administration.
Master Shot	The overall picture of the action. CLOSE-UPS and reaction shots are cut in to the master shot.
Media	From "electronic media." Radio, film and television, as opposed to stage.
Method	Lee Strasberg's development of Stanislavski's counter to the style of acting popular in Russia at the turn of the century.
Mid-Shot	(MS) Shows the human body to waist level.
Monologue	One person speaking. An audition speech is a special sort of monologue. A one-person play is a monodrama.
MOS	"Mit-out sound" (from European film directors in early Hollywood?). Mock-German description of scene shot for visuals only.
Most Favoured Nation	Undeservedly reviled contractual provision, now forbidden by Equity, in which the actor is guaranteed that nobody else in the cast is making more money.

Noddy	The familiar shot of the interviewer "reacting to" words off-screen. Recorded afterwards, it means the guest can be edited unobtrusively.
Nonprofessional Affidavit	See LOCAL JOBBER.
Nut	The weekly cost of running a show. "To make the nut" is to break even for the week. The story is that the innkeeper would keep the axle nut from a traveling show's cart until he was paid in full.
Negotiate	Not getting everything you deserve from someone who thinks you are getting too much.
Off Book	Knowing one's lines well enough to need only occasional prompting.
On Air	Broadcasting.
On Camera	In view of the video audience.
Out of Work	Not presently hired as an actor.
Pan	To rotate a camera on its mounting.
Paper	"To p. the house." To give away complimentary tickets to boost the apparent size of the paying audience.
Patch	Connect lighting circuits to the dimmer board so that one dimmer controls a group of lights.
Per Diem	Payment made to actors working out of town to cover hotel and meals.
Permittee	Actor not a member of ACTRA working for a union engager.
Personal Manager	Agent.

Post-Production   After the filming or taping is over, choosing the best parts of the takes, adding music, POST-SYNCH, to turn the raw performance material into a saleable product.

Post-Synch   (LOOPING, ADR) Adding dialogue, synchronised with the originally recorded words where necessary, after the main filming or taping is finished.

POV   Point of view. The camera shows the scene as if through a particular character's eyes.

Principal   A major character (various union definitions).

Producer   In commercial theatre and the media, one who puts together the major elements of a show and arranges the financing.
In English theatre: a director.

Production Company   In media, the concern actually making the film or TV show which other people may have conceived and commissioned.

Production Stage Manager   PSM. In large theatres, head of stage management department. Similar to COMPANY MANAGER.

Profession   The people involved in the acting business. The business itself.

Programming Agent   Your own agent, rather than the agency's specialist in, say, commercials.

Prompt   To give an actor a line he has forgotten. Rarely found in performance since the end of PROSCENIUM theatre. The hardest job for an ASM in rehearsals.

Prompt Book   The master copy of the script. "The Bible." Records final decisions on lines, moves and business, with cues for lights, sound, etc.

Prop	Property. An object, not furniture, on a set to be used. Often a fake. Personal props (cigars, whip, copy of *Buglestone Chronicle*, etc.) remain with the actor or are returned to him at the end of the show.
Proscenium	(Prosc) The wall between the stage and the audience in traditional theatre buildings. "P. theatre": such a theatre. "P. arch": the frame of the traditional stage picture.
Pro-rated	Partial payment, proportionally reduced for partial work.
PSM	PRODUCTION STAGE MANAGER.
Rake	Now mainly in older PROSCENIUM theatres, the gradient of a stage so that the rear is higher than the front, giving better acoustics and sightlines.
Regional	R. theatre; once, a theatre serving a large area by touring, etc. Now, the major professional non-profit theatre in an area. In the US, any not-for-profit theatre outside New York City.
Repertoire	(1) Past seasons' plays, which characterize the theatre. (2) The organization of a season so that a cast rehearses a group of plays, which it then performs in turn.
Repertory	(1) Now synonymous with and replacing REPERTOIRE (2). (2) In UK, a theatre producing a number of plays in an announced season.
Report	"To put on r." Doesn't exist and never did. A theatrical bugaboo to scare the children. Equity has a dispute procedure to resolve contractual problems between artist and theatre, which may result in either being penalized. This is rarely used.

Resident　　R. company. One with season-long occupancy of the same building.
R. designer, etc. A staff position, not a free lance JOBBED IN.

Residuals　　Television fees are paid partly for work done (the session fee) and partly for the use made of the final product (residuals or use fees). These are paid in advance for a period of use in a specified market and may continue for many years. Thank God.

Resting　　Word nonprofessionals use to describe actors' being OUT OF WORK.

Résumé　　One-page summary of actor's experience, skills, physical type, etc.

Retake　　In the media, to record a shot again.

Review　　Drama critic's version of what happened on first night.

Revolve　　Rotating platform, on the stage or set into it. They never work.

Right　　Stage right: actor's right, facing the audience. Camera right: actor's left, facing the camera. (Draw a moral, if you like.)

Roll　　Start camera or tape-recorder working.

Roster　　List of the actors an agent represents.

Rounds　　"Doing the r." The process of self-publicity. From New York practice of physically visiting agents, casting directors, etc., trying to catch a word of encouragement.

Run　　Vb., to rehearse a whole section of a play without stopping.
Vb., "to r. lines" – to practise scripted dialogue without moves.

N., the number of consecutive performances of a play.

Run-through   An attempt to rehearse a whole section without stopping.

Safety   Benevolent media lie: "That was perfect – let's do another TAKE, just as a safety."

SAG   Screen Actors' Guild. American film union.

Saint Genesius   Patron saint of actors.

Scrim   An open-weave material which appears solid from the lit side but disappears when the scene behind is lit instead.

Season   A group of plays announced in advance.

Second Unit   Film crew for atmosphere and crowd shooting. Often does stunt and special effects and shoots material found necessary in POST-PRODUCTION

SEG   Screen Extras Guild. American. "Central Casting, send me a dozen Pia Zadoras."

Set   In film and TV, the place where the acting takes place.
In theatre, the construction on the stage.

Shooting Ratio   Between the final length of the edited film or videotape and the amount originally shot.

Shot   (1) What is to happen between calling "action" and "CUT."
(2) The type of picture the camera is set up for. See LONG SHOT, MID-SHOT, CLOSE-UP, BIG CLOSE-UP, EXTREME CLOSE-UP.

Showcase   A stage production where all or most of the profit for the people involved, especially the actors, is in demonstrating their skills to people who may hire them.

Shutter   BARN DOOR. Hinged panel in front of the light cutting off edge of beam.

Sides   Originally theatre, now mainly media. Only those pages of the script that have a particular character's lines.

Sightline   An imaginary line from the eyes of someone in a theatre audience to a part of the stage. Particularly, the line after which you can be seen coming onto the stage. Important in designing sets and blocking so that the action can be seen, and in designing auditoriums so that all seats have a good view.

Signatory   An engager who has agreed to hire actors only under the terms of an agreement negotiated with a performers' union.

Slate   Vb. (1) Use the CLAPPER BOARD to identify a shot. (2) Identify yourself and your agent before a taped audition.

Socko   A comedy hit. From the Greek comedy actors' low soft shoe, "soccus."

Soubrette   Heroine's best friend.

Spelvin   (George, Georgina) Fictitious name used in a theatre programme to conceal the fact that an actor is playing two roles. In UK, Walter Plinge.

SRO   Traditional but rarely used sign: Standing Room Only.

Stage   (1) Theatre acting area.
                     (2) Theatre work as opposed to MEDIA.

Stage Manager   (SM) She Who Must Be Obeyed. Administers rehearsals, including breaks and overtime reports, passes on show's needs to technical departments, compiles the prompt copy. Maintains liaison between actors and management. After opening, maintains the director's show. In US, may also cast and rehearse understudies and replacements.

Stagehand   One who changes scenery and does other physical jobs backstage.

Statutory Holiday   Forget it. You don't rehearse on Christmas Day but otherwise it's business as usual.

Steadicam   Patented camera mount giving "hand-held" manoeuvrability with close to studio smoothness in movement.

Steward   ACTRA employee who polices productions, or is at least available on the phone in case of trouble.

Stock   Properly, a company or theatre which produces different plays successively without a substantial dark period or lay-off between.

Story Day   In film, TV, the passing of a day in the narrative, as opposed to time passing in the production process.

Story Board   The high points of a film, TV, story shown in sketches with key dialogue.

Strike   (1) Taking down a set at the end of a scene or more permanently when the run of a play is over.
(2) In the sense of industrial action, almost unknown. See Chapter Ten, "All for One..."

Studio   (1) Small theatre space, often a simple room with movable seating.
(2) Indoor media space devoted to recording and broadcasting.

Stumble-through An early attempt to get through a section of a play without stopping. The director wants a RUN-THROUGH but the SM knows the actors aren't up to it. A stagger-through is worse.

Succès d'Estime Everyone likes the show. No one pays to see it.

Tableau Frozen stage action. In Victorian theatre, the main curtain would be raised briefly after the end of an act to show the next exciting second.

Tabs Main curtains in a PROSCENIUM theatre. Perhaps from TABLEAU.

Take (1) Short for "double take," a familiar comedy routine.
(2) In film or TV, an attempt to record a sequence. ("Pouring the milk, take twenty-seven.")

Talent Actors, in the media.

Talent Agent Agent, personal manager, representing and paid by a roster of clients. As opposed to a CASTING AGENT, paid by the engager.

Talley Light Red light on top of the TV camera that currently has the picture on screen.

TBA To Be Announced.

Teaser Wide, short curtain hanging above the stage to mask the FLIES and light battens.

Technical Director Similar to PSM but more linked with craft departments and less with actors.

Three-Point Lighting Standard media lighting consisting of BACK LIGHT, FILL and KEY LIGHT. The key light produces highlights on your face, the fill lightens the shadows from the key, and the back light separates you from the background.

Thrust	The stage extends forward so that the first rows of the audience wrap around it.
TK	(or TC) Telecine, i.e. transferring film or projected stills to videotape.
Tormentor	The most forward wing flat or leg, closest to the PROSCENIUM.
Tracking	Moving the camera parallel to the action. On tracks, hence the name.
Trades	American expression for periodicals dealing with news of productions now being planned or in process, casting, etc. Nearest equivalent here would be *Canadian Theatre Review, Playback, Equity Newsletter* or *Theatrum* (see Addresses, page 194).
Trap	Trap door in the stage. Various designs, all dangerous.
Traveller	A stage curtain, generally large, that opens from the middle out.
Twofer	Bargain ticket – two fer the price of one.
Type	Classification of parts an actor could play.
Typecast	Given a part for which one is obviously suited.
Underdress	To wear a (part of a) costume under another, to speed a quick change.
Understudy	Actor ready (more or less) to take over a part in an emergency.
Unemployed	Not currently under contract as an actor.
Up Front	Paid in advance.

Use Fee (RESIDUAL) Part of a media fee, calculated by reference to the potential audience for a production.

Voice-over Off-camera speaker heard over action on screen. Also, loosely, narration over background sound on radio.

Walk the Stage An ASM or convenient actor moves about the acting area for the designer so that uneven lighting can be seen and corrected.

Walk in More or less unofficial equivalent to a complimentary ticket. The FOH manager may walk a person past the ticket-taker and allow the use of seats unoccupied close to curtain time.

Walk-on A theatre extra, with no personal characterisation. Talks in crowds, may have one individual line.

Walk-through A tentative run-through with limited objectives. See STUMBLE-THROUGH.

Wardrobe (1) The clothes you wear as costume.
(2) The rooms where they are made, repaired and stored.
(3) The people who do the work on the clothes.

Window Shot The last shot of the day. *Win do we* go home?

Wings Space at the side of a stage, nominally out of the audience's sight. The FLATS meant to conceal this space.

Work Permit When a non-member of ACTRA is hired for a union production, except as an extra, a fee must be paid to ACTRA. This also serves to record the job as part of the actor's qualifications to join ACTRA.

Working   Under contract as an actor.

Workshop   (1) A minimal production of a play to improve it before public showing.
(2) A class, with some practical component.

Wrangler   In media, person responsible for animals; originally horses, now also children, etc.

Wrap   Media talk for "finish with." "You're wrapped." "It's a wrap." "A wrap party."

This glossary is wrapped.

Addresses

ACTRA
(Alliance of Canadian Cinema Television and Radio Artists)
2239 Yonge Street, Toronto, Ontario M4S 2B5
Telephone: (416) 489-1311 or 1-800-387-3516

ACTRA Fraternal Benefit Society
1000 Yonge Street, Toronto, Ontario M4W 2K2
Telephone: (416) 967-6600 or 1-800-387-8897

Canada Council
Arts Award Service,
99 Metcalfe Street, Ottawa, Ontario K1P 5V8
Telephone: (613) 237-3400
Theatre Section: (613) 589-4344

Canadian Conference of the Arts
189 Laurier Avenue East, Ottawa, Ontario K1N 6P1
Telephone: (613) 238-3561
• An umbrella organization for arts groups across the country.

Canadian Theatre Review
University of Toronto Press, Journals Department
P.O. Box 1280, 1011 Sheppard Avenue West, Downsview B,
Ontario M3H 5V4
Telephone: (416) 667-7781/82
• Articles on theatre themes, new play scripts, national news.

Equity
(Canadian Actors' Equity Association)
260 Richmond Street East, Toronto, Ontario M5A 1P4
Telephone: (416) 867-9165 or 1-800-387-1856

PACT
(Professional Association of Canadian Theatres)
64 Charles Street East, Toronto, Ontario M4Y 1T1
Telephone: (416) 968-3033

Performing Arts Magazine
1100 Caledonia Road, Toronto, Ontario M6A 2W5
Telephone: (416) 785-4300

Playback
366 Adelaide Street West, Suite 500, Toronto, Ontario M5V 1R9
Telephone: (416) 408-2300
* TV/film production news.

Playwrights Union of Canada (PUC)
54 Wolseley Street, 2nd Floor, Toronto, Ontario M5T 1A5
Telephone: (416) 947-0201
* Reading room and national office. Publishes *Canplay*, a playwrights' view of theatre.

Theatrum
Box 688, Station C, Toronto M6J 3S1
Telephone: (416) 493-5740
* Alternative theatre magazine.

Union des Artistes
1290 rue Saint Denis, 6th Floor, Montreal H2X 3J7
Telephone: (514) 288-6682
Francophone performers' union.

ALBERTA

ACCESS Network
3720 – 76 Avenue, Edmonton T6B 2N9
Telephone: (403) 440-7777
* Distributor and producer of television programming and educational materials.

ACTRA
Calgary Branch: #260, 1414 – 8th Street S.W. T2R 1J6
Telephone: (403) 228-3123

Edmonton Branch: #201, 10816A – 82 Avenue T6E 2B3
Telephone: (403) 433-4090

Government of Alberta, Culture and Multiculturalism
Arts Branch
11th Floor, 10004 – 104 Avenue, Edmonton T5J 0K5
Telephone: (403) 427-2565
* Education, touring and financial assistance for individuals and organizations.

PUC Reading Rooms
Calgary: Alberta Playwrights Network
125 – 9th Avenue S.E., Calgary T2G 0P6
Telephone: (403) 269-8564

Edmonton: Theatre Alberta
19136 – 100 Street, #308 T5J 0P1
Telephone: (403) 424-0299

BRITISH COLUMBIA
ACTRA
#300, 1622 W. 7th Avenue, Vancouver V6J 1S5
Telephone: (604) 734-1414

CBC
Box 4600, Vancouver V6B 4A2
Telephone: (604) 662-6000

Duthie Books Ltd.
919 Robson Street, Vancouver V6Z 1A5
Telephone: (604) 684-4496
• Book store with excellent performing arts section.

Equity – Western Office
101 Carrall Street, Vancouver V6B 2H9
Telephone: (604) 682-6173

Ministry of Tourism, Recreation and Culture
Cultural Services Branch
600 Johnson Street, 6th Floor, Victoria V8V 1X4
Telephone: (604) 356-1718
• Grants programmes and complementary services.

PUC Reading Rooms
Vancouver: New Play Centre
1405 Anderson Street, Granville Island, Vancouver V6H 3R5
Telephone: (604) 685-6288

Victoria: Gwen Pharis Ringwood Room, University of Victoria
Box 1700, Station E, Victoria V8W 2Y2
Telephone: (604) 721-7991

Theatre B.C.
1005 Broad Street, #307, Victoria V8W 2A1
Telephone: (604) 381-2443
• Community theatre umbrella organization.

Workshops in the Performing Arts
1110 Seymour Street, #203, Vancouver V6B 3N3
Telephone: (604) 689-0772

MANITOBA

ACTRA
#110, Phoenix Building, 388 Donald Street, Winnipeg R3B 2J4
Telephone: (204) 943-1307/2365

Manitoba Arts Council
#525, 93 Lombard Avenue, Winnipeg R3B 3B1
Telephone: (204) 945-2237
• Projects grants, bursaries, artists-in-schools.

PUC Reading Room
Manitoba Association of Playwrights,
#503, 100 Arthur Street, Winnipeg R3B 1H3
Telephone: (204) 942-8941

NEW BRUNSWICK

Department of Municipalities, Culture and Housing
Arts Branch,
P.O. Box 6000, Fredericton E3B 5H1
Telephone: (506) 453-3610
• Financial assistance to artists for development, travel, artists-in-schools.

PUC Reading Room
University of New Brunswick,
229 Carlton Hall, Fredericton E3B 5A3
Telephone: (506) 453-4676

NEWFOUNDLAND

ACTRA
Newfoundland & Labrador Branch,
210 Water Street, St. John's A1C 5K8
Telephone: (709) 722-0430

Newfoundland and Labrador Arts Council
P.O. Box 5011, St. John's A1C 5V3
Telephone: (709) 726-2212
• Direct grants, loans, loan subsidies, awards.

PUC Reading Room
Writers' Alliance of Newfoundland and Labrador
127 Queens Road, St. John's A1C 2B4
Telephone: (709) 739-5215

NOVA SCOTIA

ACTRA
Maritimes Branch,
5510 Spring Garden Road, Halifax B3J 1G5
Telephone: (902) 420-1404

Department of Tourism and Culture
Performing Arts Division
P. O. Box 864, Halifax B3J 2V2
Telephone: (902) 424-4378
• Supports visiting guest artists, travel assistance to upgrade
skills, plus theatre and play grants.

PUC Reading Room
Department of Tourism and Culture
1601 Lower Water Street, 4th Floor, Halifax B3J 3C6
Telephone: (902) 424-5000

ONTARIO

ACTRA
Toronto Branch : 2239 Yonge Street M4S 2B5
Telephone: (416) 489-1311
Hotline: (416) 483-7494

Ottawa Branch: #808, 130 Slater Street K1P 6E2
Telephone: (613) 230-0327/8

ALAS (Artists' Legal Advice Service)
Toronto: 183 Bathurst Street M5T 2R7
Telephone: (416) 360-0772

Ottawa: 189 Laurier Avenue East K1N 6P1
Telephone: (613) 567-2690

CBC
Canadian Broadcasting Corporation,
Box 500, Station A, Toronto M5W 1E6
Talent Resource Centre: (416) 205-7201
TV Drama Casting: (416) 205-7190
Radio Drama Casting: (416) 205-6011

Equity Showcase
221 Dufferin Street, #308A, Toronto M6K 1Y9
Telephone: (416) 533-6100
• Classes in theatre skills, special events, Showcase Production series.

Samuel French
80 Richmond Street East, Toronto M5C 1P1
Telephone: (416) 363-3536
• Large stock of mainly standard plays, very cheap.

Galbraith Reproductions Ltd.
201 Dufferin Street, Toronto M6K 1Y9
Telephone: (416) 531-6913

Graphic Artists
58 Stewart Street, Toronto M5V 1H6
Telephone: (416) 362-0737
• Has a mailing service across Canada for photo reproductions.

Metro Toronto Reference Library
789 Yonge Street, Toronto M4W 2G8
Arts, telephone: (416) 393-7077
General Reference, telephone: (416) 393-7131

Ontario Arts Council
151 Bloor Street W,, #500, Toronto M5S 1T6
Telephone: (416) 961-1660
• Supports theatre organizations and new works by emerging
  companies and co-operatives.

PUC Reading Rooms
Toronto: Playwrights Union of Canada
54 Wolseley Street, 2nd floor M5T 1A5
Telephone: (416) 947-0201

Thunder Bay: Thunder Bay Public Library
Brodie Resource Department,
Thunder Bay P7E 3L6
Telephone: (807) 623-0925

Theatre Centre
1032 Queen Street West, Toronto M6J 1H7
Telephone: (416) 538-0988
• Umbrella organization of alternative theatres.

Theatre Ontario
6th Floor, 344 Bloor Street W., Toronto M5S 3A7
Telephone: (416) 964-6771
• Major information source on professional non-union theatre
  (and media), as well as community theatre. Talent Bank,
  magazine; office has essential notice boards.

Theatrebooks
11 St. Thomas Street, Toronto M5S 2B7
Telephone: (416) 922-7175
• Canadian theatre section. Helpful staff, large stock. Theatre
  and media books, etc. Has an excellent mail order service.

Toronto Arts Council
141 Bathurst Street, Toronto M5V 2R2
Telephone: (416) 392-6800

Toronto Association of Acting Studios
6th Floor, 344 Bloor Street W., Toronto M5S 3A7
Telephone: (416) 964-6771
• Information about member's classes.

Toronto Theatre Alliance
720 Bathurst Street, Toronto M5S 2R4
Telephone: (416) 536-6468
- Service organization for professional theatre and dance companies. Activities include lobbying and advocacy for small theatres, co-operative buying and professional development.

TV Ontario
2180 Yonge Street, Toronto M4S 2B9
Telephone: (416) 484-2600
- Family and educational programming. Some production.

Union des Artistes
Ontario Branch, #206, 2 College Street, Toronto M5G 1K3
Telephone: (416) 967-4408

PRINCE EDWARD ISLAND
Council of the Arts
P.O. Box 2234, 94 Great George Street, Charlottetown C1A 4K4
Telephone: (902) 368-4410
- Individual grants, workshops, travel and study grants.

PUC Reading Room
Confederation Centre Library,
Box 7000, Charlottetown C1A 8G8
Telephone: (902) 368-4642

QUEBEC
ACTRA
#530, 1450 City Councillors Street, Montreal H3A 2E6
Telephone: (514) 844-3318

PUC Reading Room
Playwrights' Workshop,
3680 Jeanne Mance, #310, Montreal H2X 2K5
Telephone: (514) 843-3685

Quebec Drama Federation
4001 rue Berri, 2nd Floor, Montreal H2L 4H2
Telephone: (514) 843-8698
Hotline: (514) 843-2873
- The Hotline has details of anglo theatre currently running. *QDF Updates* has news of anglo theatre and classes.

Union des Artistes
National Office: 1290 Rue Saint Denis, 6th Floor, Montreal H2X 3J7
Telephone: (514) 288-6682

Quebec City: 580 avenue Grand Allée est G1R 2K2
Telephone: (418) 523-4241

SASKATCHEWAN

ACTRA
Saskatchewan Branch: #212, 1808 Smith Street, Regina S4P 2N4
Telephone: (306) 757-0885

PUC Reading Room
Saskatchewan Playwrights Centre
Suite 719, Bessborough Hotel, 601 Spadina Crescent East,
Saskatoon S7K 3G8
Telephone: (306) 665-7707

Saskatchewan Arts Board
3475 Albert Street, 3rd Floor, Regina S4S 6X6
Telephone: (306) 787-4056
Toll-free in Saskatchewan: 1-800-667-7526
- Individual grants for theatre training.

Saskatchewan Film Pool
1100 Broad Street, Regina S4R 6V7
Telephone: (306) 757-8818
- Source of non-union film casting information.

YUKON

Yukon Arts Council
4061 – 4th Avenue, P.O. Box 5120, Whitehorse Y1A 4S3
Telephone: (403) 668-6284
- Also has PUC Reading Room.